EDITED BY **CRAIG BARTON**
SERIES EDITOR **TOM BENNETT**

THE research ✎**ED** GUIDE TO

EDUCATION MYTHS

AN EVIDENCE-INFORMED
GUIDE FOR TEACHERS

First Published 2019

by John Catt Educational Ltd,
15 Riduna Park, Station Road,
Melton, Woodbridge IP12 1QT

Tel: +44 (0) 1394 389850
Email: enquiries@johncatt.com
Website: www.johncatt.com

ISBN: 978 1 912906 39 0

Set and designed by John Catt Educational Limited

WHAT IS researchED?

researchED is an international, grassroots education-improvement movement that was founded in 2013 by Tom Bennett, a London-based high school teacher and author. researchED is a truly unique, teacher-led phenomenon, bringing people from all areas of education together onto a level playing field. Speakers include teachers, principals, professor, researchers and policy makers.

Since our first sell-out event, researchED has spread all across the UK, into the Netherlands, Norway, Sweden, Australia, the USA, with events planned in Spain, Japan, South Africa and more. We hold general days as well as themed events, such as researchED Maths & Science, or researchED Tech.

WHO ARE WE?

Since 2013, researchED has grown from a tweet to an international conference movement that so far has spanned six continents and thirteen countries. We have simple aims: to help teaching become more evidence-facing; to raise the reserach literacy in teaching; to improve education research standards; and to bring research users and research creators closer together. To do this, we hold unique one-day conferences that bring together teachers, researchers, academics and anyone touched by research. We believe in teacher voice, and short-circuiting the top-down approach to education that benefits no one.

HOW DOES IT WORK?

The gathering of mainly teachers, researchers, school leaders, policymakers and edu-bloggers creates a unique dynamic. Teachers and researchers can attend the sessions all day and engage with each other to exchange ideas. The vast majority of speakers stay for the duration of the conference, visit each other's sessions, work on the expansion of their knowledge and gain a deeper understanding of the work of their peers. Teachers can take note of recent developments in educational research, but are also given the opportunity to provide feedback on the applicability of research or practical obstacles.

CONTENTS

FOREWORD:
EDUMYTHS AND
THE SLEEP OF REASON

What is a myth? A story; a legend; a folk tale, especially one that has explanatory power for phenomena that people cannot otherwise understand or interpret. Before we understood thunder, Norsemen ascribed its boom to the hooves of Sleipnir, Thor's eight-legged steed. Apollo raced his golden chariot across the sky to bring us sunrise and sunset.

Later mythologies added infinite variety. By the time we reach St Aquinas, we no longer see the planets as celestial fireflies, but as heavenly bodies, their motion explained by the will of God and Natural Law. We call this phenomenon the 'God of the gaps'. For every unexplained event, we point to God and say 'He did it.' As our knowledge of the natural universe expanded, the gaps in our knowledge shrunk; but there were always gaps. And wherever there were gaps, God was there, explaining everything.

Now that we have mapped so much of the everyday, sub-atomic and galactic realms, now that Einstein and Newton and Bohr and so many others have started to sketch the tracks on which the world runs, we see the supernatural in the physical gaps less frequently. And when an explanation is lacking, we usually assume a natural one will be found. Only in the discourse of the habitually religious do we see people routinely ascribing the hand of God to surprising recoveries from previously interminable and terminal illness, for instance.

What we do still see is the habitual response to ascribe supernatural explanations to uncharted territories.

Goya's famous etching *The Sleep of Reason Produces Monsters* holds up a mirror to this process. In the absence of reason and evidence, we conjure up absurd explanations and superstitions. Walking under ladders, lucky horseshoes, the nervous student's mascot, saluting magpies are all common, apparently harmless superstitions, perhaps some kind of mechanism by which we displace anxiety by symbolically restoring some semblance of control over situations that frighten us.

Education is full of myths. No – education is built on them, as many cultures are, and is currently in the grip of a mythomania so pronounced that we might declare it a golden age for neopagan mythology. When I trained to teach in 2003, I assumed, not unreasonably, that the methods in which I was trained, and the pedagogy that was being directly imparted to me, would be based on the most evidenced and robust bases of knowledge and reason we possessed. I assumed that, given we had been educating our children since prehistory, it would be a field in which most of the great debates would have been amicably resolved for some time, in the same way as we had long-since settled the matter about what the shortest distance between two points should be.

I was hopelessly wrong. The field I entered was as contested and unhappy as you could imagine. Not that you would have known it from my induction to the profession, where I rarely heard a whisper that there was any debate at all. As far as I knew by that point, education was indeed an uncontested field.

And yet. I trained on a long-since discontinued programme called Fast Track during the prodigious era of Tony Blair's premiership, when UK education swam in money. Part of my boutique, and expensive training, consisted of week-long residentials learning the art and craft of teaching through such things as neuro-linguistic programming (NLP), learning styles, multiple intelligences, and a host of other fashionable follies about how the brain learned. We absorbed it breathlessly, excited to be part of such a glittering future.

The problem was, it was all junk. NLP, learning styles, all of it. Pseudoscience at best, speckled with a seasoning of real science to make it smell right. As I progressed in my career, a terrible Damascene conversion overtook me: much of what we had been told, and a great deal of our training, was simply wrong. Which isn't to say the people promoting it were charlatans, or insincere. They were simply mistaken, or careless, or their reason slept.

Some of it was simply garbage, such as learning styles – not even wrong. Other parts of it were like the fetishes in religion, celebrated with reverence for powers they never possessed: group work, for example, was sold to a generation of teachers as the highest, 'deepest' form of instruction, along with project work, thematic learning, flipped learning and a hundred other varieties of student-led enquiry. Now, these pedagogies aren't, strictly speaking, junk science – in fact in many contexts they are very useful tools – but the way they were over-sold was as if they were innately and intrinsically superior. A generation of teachers tried to make every lesson about group work, or set witless independent tasks that many students were not qualified to undertake.

Why is this? One reason is that educational research is notoriously hard to do well – and often expensive. Any study of human behaviour is. And any study of human behaviour at scale is harder still. Human psychology is famously resistant to sitting still and being observed, unlike water molecules. It is incredibly hard to say anything of any level of certainty about human behaviour. The further back you pull from the individual, the more reliable the prediction for the group, but the less you can predict the behaviour of any one of them.

Another is that the education sector is frequently dominated by a priesthood of gatekeepers and institutions that now apparently exists solely to sustain and congratulate themselves. Fashionable philosophies from the 19th century were adopted wholesale by generations of educationalists who felt that their ideologies need not be exposed to examination, or the need to demonstrate validity in real classrooms. Evidence, in this model, is seen as an irritant, contradicting the hypothetical models of academia. If real schools seemed immune to improvement through this kind of magic thinking, then the evidence must be wrong, and the schools must be doing it wrong. Sadly, this kind of thinking has long-since worked its way into a great deal of teacher induction, which replicated and sustained many of the myths for generation after generation of teacher.

Another is simply that there is often no personal cost for being wrong in education. If you want to claim, as many have, that tablets will revolutionise teaching, and you are fortunate to have a budget to buy one for every pupil in the city, then by the time your belief is tested in reality, the likelihood is that you will no longer hold the office that entitled you to do so. Any failure can be ascribed to improper implementation, or a thousand other factors. Of course, there are multiple real costs in getting things wrong in education, but the bearers of these costs – the students, and indirectly their teachers – rarely get a say in what happens to them, and the tax payers rarely appreciate the vast bonfire that was made of their contributions.

This is a miserable place to find ourselves, in a sector so important, so expensive, and so intimately linked to our collective ambitions and dreams for the future. Or perhaps I should say it was. Because there is a burgeoning counter-culture now emerging that seeks to defy this culture. An international community of teachers, educationalists, teacher trainers, policy makers, academics and researchers who are no longer content to accept this broken, brutal model for children or themselves. Just as our ancestors started to find answers in empirical science that led us to Wi-Fi and interplanetary travel and bifocal lenses, so too are educators of all stripes starting to collaborate meaningfully in a global reinvention of what and how we teach.

researchED has, I hope, been a small part of this process. Started in 2013, I wanted to try to catalyse and nurture the green shoots of rebirth that I sensed around the birth of social media, surely one of the midwives to this process. We've encouraged an iconoclastic bonfire of much of what precedes us in education. As Hume would say, let us consign them to the flames. We encourage a philosophical suspension of disbelief about as many claims as possible. We avoid certainty, and embrace context. When researchED started we used the tagline 'Working out what works'. We didn't mean that we thought this was easy, or the answers were simple, or neat, or certain.

For teachers, working out what works matters. It doesn't mean that any given strategy succeeds in every condition or circumstance. Some strategies will have higher probabilities than others. Some will fail despite high likelihoods of success. That's fine. Certainty is overrated. And while education research may never approach the validity or reliability that many of the physical sciences offer us, it gets us a hell of a lot closer to what we need to do than prayer-based education, good intentions, and happy thoughts, which is where we often find ourselves.

This book explores some – not all – of the myths that have found a home in education. It also explores some of the reasons why such myths are allowed to grow and flourish. Nothing here is incontestable. Many of the points raised are supported rather than proven. That's the point: a professional community of educators looks at the best available evidence bases and maps that onto the structured analyses of professional experience, and attempts to reconcile the two. This overlap of craft and science is, for me, the sweet spot, and exactly where we need to be. Embracing uncertainty with the best tools we have, not leaping into the darkness. Our torches may flicker and seem dim at times. But a little light is all we need.

I hope you enjoy this book, the first in a series, that you find it useful, and a catalyst for your own thinking and development. Nothing here is incontestable. Nothing here is sacred. That's the point.

Tom Bennett
Founder, researchED
Series editor

INTRODUCTION

BY CRAIG BARTON

Education is awash with myths.

At the risk of starting this book with a ridiculously early plug, my first book, *How I Wish I'd Taught Maths* (available from all good – and all evil – bookstores) is essentially a sordid tale of how myths plagued my teaching for 12 years. Learning styles, learning by discovery, an obsession with engagement, group work every lesson, fear of teacher talk – the list goes on. Some of what I now consider to be myths were explicitly presented to me as facts by authority figures. Others – and I now think these are the most dangerous – were rarely spoken about or questioned. They became the norms that my colleagues and I accepted. They were, quite simply, the only way to do things.

It took 200 research papers, 25 books, over 100 hours of conversation with experts from around the world, and 140,000 words of soul-searching to question all the practices and beliefs I held dear in that first book. And to be honest, I had hoped I was done. But in the 18 months since my book's release, I find myself contemplating a few other 'truths' about my classroom practice.

Here are three for starters:

1. Student discussion is always a good thing

One of the misconceptions some people have about the model of teaching I describe in my first book – especially when it comes to my use of 'silent teacher'[1] – is that my students do not utter a word for hours on end.

This is not true. Whilst I certainly do make much more use of focused periods of silence than I used to – both during my modelling of a worked example, and for portions of time when students are working on problems – I regularly encourage my students to collaborate and learn from each other. Students engaged in positive debate and discussion as they attempt to thrash out a problem is a wonderful sight.

But are such discussions *always* a good thing?

---

1. Silent teacher is covered in chapters 4 and 6 of *How I Wish I'd Taught Maths.*

Obviously we could have problems with focus and behaviour. If discussions stray away from quadratic equations towards the direction of *Love Island*,[2] then the effect on learning is likely to be negative. But even if students remain on task, and all discussions are purely mathematical, then my further reading of the 'self-explanation effect' – something that played a key role in my first book[3] – suggests something else I need to bear in mind.

Chi (2000) explains that 'self-explaining is a knowledge-building activity that is generated by and directed to oneself'. In a 2018 meta-analysis, Bisra et al. conclude that 'the process of self-explanation also helps the learner realise what they don't know, to fill in missing information, monitor understanding, and modify fusions of new information with prior knowledge when discrepancies or deficiencies are detected'.

Self-explaining is powerful, and is a key behaviour I want my students to develop. But it is also something that could be jeopardised by student discussion.

Imagine you are thinking really hard about a problem. The pieces are starting to come together in your mind. You are nearly there. Just a few more seconds…and then the person next to you tells you how to do it. This is not only extremely annoying, but also potentially detrimental to your learning. Your opportunity to fill in missing information, modify fusions of new knowledge, and all the other wonderful things Bisra et al. describe are taken away.

The problem with discussion – whether it be in pairs, groups, or whole class – is that it does not allow individuals to make connections at the point that they are ready. In a sense, you are at the behest of the person in the group that understands the current problem the quickest. And with everyone quite naturally gripping ideas and concepts at different points in time, this is clearly an issue.

The solution I am currently pondering may cause readers to throw this book on the floor in disgust.

With several classes I have adopted the '4-2 approach', in which students first work for four minutes in silence, and then for the next two minutes they discuss with their partner, then four minutes' silence, two minutes' discussion – and the cycle continues.

---

2. If you do not know what *Love Island* is, my advice is to keep it that way.

3. The self-explanation effect is covered in chapter 5 of *How I Wish I'd Taught Maths*.

My hope is that this structure allows my students to benefit from a dedicated period of focused work where they can tap into the benefits of the self-explanation effect and the testing effect[4], and then really make the most of their discussion time at a point when they have had the opportunity to put many of the pieces together themselves.

It is early days in my experimentation with the 4-2 approach, but the signs are promising.

2. Students learn from each other's answers

A mistake I made for many years was making an inference about the understanding of a class based on the answers of one or two students. In the early days of my career I would commit the cardinal sin of asking a question and waiting for a hand to go up, and then feel content with my wonderful teaching because the smartest, most confident student in the class had got it right. As I got a little bit better, I would start to employ techniques like Doug Lemov's 'cold call',[5] whereby I took control over which students would answer each question.

However, a 2018 study by Abel and Roediger suggests an issue that I had somewhat overlooked. In a series of three experiments, participants worked together in restudy and retrieval practice of vocabulary pairs. One subject acted as a speaker whilst the other listened and monitored their partner's response. The authors found that the subject speaking remembered more in a subsequent test than the subject listening, unless the subject listening was asked to monitor their own retrieval instead of their partner's.

The authors conclude that retrieval is not necessarily as beneficial to listeners as it is to those speaking. They go further and suggest that 'teachers asking questions in class will not yield a positive effect unless measures are taken to insure students' effortful covert retrieval'.

It seems students learn from each other's answers, but not as much as I had thought.

And so, whilst my shift to cold call when asking questions is certainly an improvement, unless I can create conditions under which every student

---

4. The testing effect is the finding that long-term memory is often increased when some of the learning period is devoted to retrieving the to-be-remembered information. There are loads of studies that find significant benefits of testing over restudy of the material. The 2011 Karpicke and Blunt study in the References is one of my favourites.

5. *Cold call*, along with a whole host of other practical classroom techniques, can be found in Doug Lemov's book, *Teach like a Champion 2.0.*

is actively trying to retrieve the answer to my question, even if the child I select explains the correct answer beautifully, it may not benefit their classmates as much, even if they listen attentively. So, my all-too-common questioning strategy of 'Josh, what do you think? ... Jenny, do you agree?' may well only benefit Josh and Jenny.

Of course, that is the key to a successful use of cold call – ensuring every student is engaged in the questioning process, thinking hard about the answer. When combined with 'no opt-out' – another strategy from Doug Lemov's *Teach like a Champion 2.0* – we begin to instil a classroom culture in which every question should benefit every student, and not just those answering them.

An alternative, of course, is to use something like diagnostic questions,[6] where every single student in the class must not only think about the answer to a question, but also show their answer. I spent an entire chapter of my last book banging on about diagnostic questions,[7] so before I get carried away again, we best move on...

3. 'Does anybody have any questions?' is a good question

I have asked my students some bad questions in my time. 'Are you happy with adding fractions?', followed by a request to indicate their joy (or lack of it) with a sea of thumbs up, down or in the middle – like a roomful of Caesars passing judgement on a defeated gladiator – was a particular low point that lasted about 12 years.

In my first book I delve into the many issues with questions like these, the most notable of which is that they are assessing confidence, not understanding, and there is by no means a perfect correlation between the two.[8]

Whilst this question has finally been dropped from my repertoire, one that has remained is 'Does anybody have any questions?' This would

---

6. See diagnosticquestions.com

7. Diagnostic questions and formative assessment are covered in chapter 11 of *How I Wish I'd Taught Maths*.

8. At the time of writing, my colleague and co-founder of *Diagnostic Questions*, Dr Simon Woodhead, is analysing over 10,000 student responses on diagnostic questions, comparing their success rate across all the questions they have answered with their confidence level on those questions. Initial findings suggest the correlation is positive but by no means perfect, with a correlation coefficient of 0.53 and key instances of over- and under-confidence. Interestingly, when we break it down by gender we find that both girls and boys overestimate their ability, but boys do this by an average of 5% more. We hope to publish these findings in the near future.

normally be unleashed at the end of a worked example, or following the completion of an exercise or activity.

What I now find myself pondering is not the question itself, but my reaction if silence follows. I would take silence as a sign of understanding. There are no questions; therefore everyone gets it, so let's crack on.

Now I am not so sure. Silence *could* indicate a complete understanding. But it could also hide one or two students who – for a variety of reasons, including confidence and anxiety – do not wish to voice their confusion. It is too easy for students to opt out of a question like this.

Moreover, silence could indicate a widespread lack of understanding across the class. It takes a certain amount of knowledge to be able to formulate a question. Someone who, for example, can articulate a question about a worked example probably understands the majority of the process, but just needs clarity on one or two aspects. The person who understands nothing does not know where to begin asking for help.

There are two solutions to this that I am currently trialling.

At the risk of sounding like a broken record, the first is to move towards questions which give me (and my students) a more accurate indication of their levels of understanding, and ensure as wide a participation rate as possible. Once again, diagnostic questions fit the bill for me.

The second is a simple tweak. Instead of asking 'Does anybody have any questions?', I now say 'Ask me a question' or – better still – 'Ask me two questions.'

This seems to elicit a greater frequency and quality of questions than my previous attempt. I think it is something to do with the fact that it is a command – 'Ask me!' – as opposed to the much weaker 'Does anybody…?' Also, the fact that I am asking for two questions means that any obvious question or feature is quickly dealt with, and then students have to think hard about the second.

Again, it is early days in my experimenting with this, but things are looking up.

Are these three things really myths? Will my proposed solutions work? I don't know. I will need to read lots more research, speak to lots of colleagues, and conduct lots more micro-experiments with different students in different contexts to be able to say so with any conviction. But these are certainly the questions that are keeping me awake at night – along with the cries of my six-month-old son. (Indeed, the latter often provides welcome relief.)

But one person, with my limited experience, can only scratch the surface of the murky world of education myths. To really get into the weeds and to understand the cause, effect and remedy for such myths, we need a team. And what a team we have.

Across eight chapters you will hear from nine of my favourite people (I managed to get a 2-for-1 deal with the Bjorks) giving their take on an array of what they consider to be education myths.

We have Mark Enser discussing the origin of myths and providing a warning for the future. Clare Sealy addresses the issues of memorable classroom experiences. Doug Lemov tackles the effect technology is having on reading. Greg Ashman delves into the world of differentiation. Robert and Elizabeth Bjork investigate the effectiveness of blocked practice. Tom Sherrington takes on student-led versus teacher-led learning. Andrew Old shares his views on attachment. Finally Harry Fletcher-Wood offers advice about changing people's practice and beliefs.

You will not agree with all the arguments presented in this book. I certainly don't. But hopefully, like me, they will make you think. I spent far too long teaching blind – accepting what I was told, what I thought, and what I perceived to be the common consensus without question. Challenging education myths is tiring, can lead to some real soul-searching, and is ultimately difficult. But we are in the business of helping to shape the lives of the young people we are lucky enough to teach. And when given a responsibility as precious as that, we do not really have a choice.

So, sit back, relax, and if not the myth-busting, at least let the *myth-confronting* begin.

References

Abel, M. and Roediger, H. L. (2018) 'The testing effect in a social setting: does retrieval practice benefit a listener?', *Journal of Experimental Psychology: Applied* 24 (3) pp. 347–359.

Barton, C. (2018) *How I wish I'd taught maths: lessons learned from research, conversations with experts, and 12 years of mistakes.* Woodbridge: John Catt Educational Limited.

Bisra, K., Liu, Q., Nesbit, J. C., Salimi, F. and Winne, P. H. (2018) 'Inducing self-explanation: a meta-analysis', *Educational Psychology Review* 30 (3) pp. 703–725.

Chi, M. T. H. (2000) 'Self-explaining: the dual processes of generating inference and repairing mental models' in Glaser, R. (ed.) *Advances in instructional psychology: educational design and cognitive science* (Vol. 5). Abingdon: Routledge, pp. 161-238.

Karpicke, J. D. and Blunt, J. R. (2011) 'Retrieval practice produces more learning than elaborative studying with concept mapping', *Science* 331 (6018) pp. 772–775.

Lemov, D. (2015) *Teach like a champion 2.0: 62 techniques that put students on the path to college.* Hoboken, NJ: John Wiley & Sons.

Author bio-sketch:
Craig Barton is a maths teacher from the North West of England. He is the maths adviser for *Tes*, creator of several websites – including diagnosticquestions.com and variationtheory.com – the author of the best-selling book *How I Wish I'd Taught Maths*, and the host of the *Mr Barton Maths* podcast. On Twitter he is @mrbartonmaths.

EDUCATION MYTHS: AN ORIGIN STORY

BY MARK ENSER

At the time of writing, I have not been lucky enough to meet Mark Enser face to face, but he has been one of the most significant influences on my thinking. Via his contributions to *Tes* and his book, *Making Every Geography Lesson Count* (AKA 'the only geography book I've ever read'), he questions, challenges and inspires.

In this chapter, Mark considers the origins of education myths, and what we can learn from past mistakes. Fretting about too much teacher talk, the willingness to spice up lessons with things like carousel tasks, and an obsession with demonstrating progress are just some of the things I embraced early in my career, only to question later. But then Mark turns his attention to retrieval quizzes, knowledge organisers, whole-class feedback, and more as he considers whether a new breed of education myths are in danger of being born out of well-founded ideas.

All villains need a compelling origin story. The Joker fell into a vat of chemical sludge; Magneto's family were killed by Nazis; Lex Luthor's work (and his hair) was destroyed by Superman. They all have a tale to tell and they tend to share certain characteristics (beginning as a victim, hurt or at least not saved by the hero they will come to battle; starting as an underdog in a cruel system). The same is true for the supervillain in our education classroom: the education myth.

Like all good origin stories, the beginnings of the many myths that assault our practice are complex and varied but there are certain common characteristics that we can explore to help us understand them better.

The mists of time

The origins of some education myths are deeply ideological. In *Getting it Wrong From the Beginning*, professor of education Kieran Egan examines the influences of the progressive educational ideology (Egan, 2002). He charts a direct link from the writing of Rousseau – and in particular his book *Emile* (Rousseau, 1921) – to the fathers of progressive education like Spencer and Dewey. In *Emile*, Rousseau warns against teachers being a figure of authority with expertise and knowledge to pass on. Instead, he insists, teachers should only be on hand to guide their pupil as they discover for themselves all they need to know, led by their own natural curiosity and at their own pace.

In *Seven Myths About Education*, former teacher Daisy Christodoulou shows that these ideas of Rousseau didn't only influence early progressive thinkers but continues to have an influence today (Christodoulou, 2014). One place we see this is in the pernicious education myth that teachers need to limit their time talking, being told things like 'If you're talking, they're not learning' or that they should be a 'guide on the side' rather than a 'sage on the stage'. It was this ideology that led to the 'learning pyramid', a distortion of Edgar Dale's work on authentic experience, to which were attached suspiciously round numbers claiming things like the 'fact' that we only remember 5% of what we are told but 90% of what we do (Harvard, 2017).

As with so many education myths, there is a kernel of truth beneath the distortions. Poor teacher explanation is hard to remember. If someone goes off on a tangent, mumbles, includes too much information in one go, it will be problematic. Recognising this gives two options:

- Firstly we could train teachers better in how to explain things clearly and in a memorable way.

- Secondly, we could create an education myth that there is something inherently wrong with teachers explaining things.

If you have an ideological view that is troubled by the idea of the teacher as an authority figure and a belief that children learn best through discovering things for themselves, you will opt for the second option. And this appears to be what happened. From these mists of time, a gang of education-myth supervillains were born: 'Limit teacher talk!', 'Pupils learn best through discovery!' and the 'guide on the side' to name but three.

Cargo cult

Many myths in education originate when some kind of strategy or technique becomes divorced from the rationale behind it. This leads to cargo cults.

The phenomenon of the cargo cult was first observed on some of the islands of the South Pacific. The islanders here wanted to attract the goods they had seen arrive by planes, brought over by Europeans and Americans. A religion grew up on these islands around rituals designed to attract the wealth back to the islands and the people built airstrips and planes from trees and made the sound of the planes they associated with the arrival of cargo (Worsley, 2009). The underlying reasons for the arrival of the cargo were gone and all that remained were their superficial structures. Doomed to failure.

The story of the cargo cult has always resonated with me as a teacher and I think we can see parallels when we start thinking about some of the ways we have been encouraged to teach in the past and with some of the things being held up as the 'next big thing' today. Take carousel tasks as an example.

Carousel tasks can work in a few different ways but they usually involve pupils working in groups on different tasks, or collecting different information, at different stations. After a certain amount of time they stop doing what they were doing at one station and move on to the next. Often there is a final step where pupils form a different group to share what they have learnt. These tasks have a number of potential issues built in to the structure that could cause concern:

- Firstly, it is likely that there is an optimal order for the information to be presented in. We usually need to know something to best make sense of something else; but in the case of the carousel, we have no control of the order in which pupils consider different aspects of the topic.

- Secondly, we either have to explain what we want pupils to do at each station at the start of the task and hope they can hold all this information in their working memory throughout the lesson or we have to hope our written instructions are clear enough at each station. There is a reason we usually communicate with our classes verbally though. It allows us to check for understanding and pick up on nonverbal cues that indicate they are not following us.

- Thirdly, time is lost in the lesson when moving from place to place. It would be a more efficient use of the time for pupils to stay in place and for the information or tasks, along with any instructions, to be given to them in sequence.

- Finally, when pupils come back together at the end to share what they have learnt, it is very easy for errors and misconceptions to be passed on unnoticed. It is almost impossible for the teacher to check understanding during this sort of task so there is very little quality control in terms of what is being passed on.

And yet these kinds of carousel tasks were always being recommended when I started teaching as a way to improve a lesson – and are still one of the first things to be suggested when a teacher asks for ideas for a lesson on social media. There may once have been an excellent rationale for the carousel task – something that addressed these problems and that explained why it was better for them to roam the room rather than be presented with the things they needed in order, but if there was, it now seems to be lost. And yet the structure remains.

What has been somewhat heartbreaking (if fascinating) to watch in recent years is the way new ideas have quickly emerged only to descend quickly into cargo-cult teaching. An example of this is the rise of the retrieval quiz at the start of a lesson. There are many good reasons to start a lesson with a recap quiz of previous learning:

- We want pupils to realise where today's lesson fits into the big picture so they can make connections between different things we have taught them (Rosenshine, 2012).

- Low-stakes tests like quizzes help pupils to remember what they have been taught for longer, even in the stressful conditions of a test (Smith et al., 2016).

- These quizzes don't only help them remember the exact thing they have been asked about but also improve their ability to answer questions only indirectly linked to the material being tested (Karpicke and Grimaldi, 2012).

- If pupils know they will be tested on something it helps to motivate them to actually learn it (Roediger et al., 2011).

- It is useful to start a lesson with a routine so that everyone knows what they are meant to be doing.

All very good reasons to start the lesson with a quiz, but what happens when we divorce the quiz from this rationale? If we don't know that a quiz can help connect different parts of a topic then why not just select quiz questions at random? If we don't know that even the effort of trying to recall an answer makes it easier to remember in the future, then why not make the questions really easy as a boost to pupil motivation? If we think the quiz is *only* a settling task then why not quiz them on what they watched on TV last night?

It isn't only happening with retrieval quizzes. We can see it with knowledge organisers too. These can be useful tools when created by a department as it helps them to think about what they are teaching and how it is best structured

(Brunskill and Enser, 2017). They can then be used by pupils as a crib sheet too: they can reflect on the key knowledge that needs to be learnt to better aid their understanding. For any of this to work, the knowledge organiser and the individual curriculum of a school need to be intertwined. And yet teachers are increasingly told they need to have these organisers but given no real reason why and so simply find one online. These then gather dust, useless and unused – like a plane made of branches on a South Pacific island.

The use of whole-class feedback is also at risk of becoming an education myth through the structure replacing the thought. The idea of whole-class feedback is very simple. Rather than writing 'You need to add more detail' in red pen in 30 exercise books, you simply tell the class this is what they need to do and show them how, then give them some way of practising doing it. Teachers have always done whole-class feedback but without needing a term for it. It was just a part of teaching.

One innovation used by some teachers was to keep a piece of paper next to their pile of exercise books so that as they were going through them they could make a note of common errors or examples of great work to share. These pieces of paper became handy templates that teachers could share, with different boxes to record information in. So far, so good. Grassroots initiatives to make teaching more effective and efficient. Unfortunately, in some schools, this template is becoming what whole-class feedback *is*. It has become a structure. A sheet to fill in and photocopy and that can be stuck in a pupil's book as evidence that feedback was given. This will become just as time consuming as individual written comments and it won't be long before teachers look at these templates and think 'Why don't I just write "Add more detail" in each book instead?' The structure kills the idea and the idea is lost.

Understanding the *why* of a strategy we deploy in the classroom is vital if we are to avoid creating new cargo-cult practices and education myths.

Desirable but impossible

Education myths can also be born out of a desire to achieve the impossible. There are many things that we would really like to be able to do, and sometimes we pretend that we can rather than admit that we can't.

One example would be the myth that we can see pupil progress and use it to make a prediction about whether they will achieve a certain GCSE grade. It would be brilliant if we could. That information would be of a huge help to pupils and parents in helping to plan for the future and school leaders could use it to plan much more targeted intervention. Sadly, it isn't really possible.

To predict where they were going to end up, it would help to know where they are now in terms of a GCSE grade. However the only way to do this would be for them to complete previous exam papers in the exact same conditions they were originally sat in (Allen, 2018). If you change the conditions (reduce the number of topics to be examined; give hints as to what to revise; reduce the number of other subjects they are revising for at the same time) you would end up with different grade boundaries.

Secondly, even if you knew where pupils currently were, progress doesn't follow nice linear routes (Treadaway, 2015). Some might make very rapid progress from this point on whereas others might plateau. Looking at the work a pupil has done in Year 10 and making a prediction about where they will be at the end of Year 11 is impossible.

And yet we ignore the fact that it is impossible because being able to do it would be so desirable. We want it badly enough that we create reporting systems and accountability systems that rely on it being done. This education myth creates the need for endless data-drops and discussions about what the predictions might mean for the school come results day in August – as though they meant anything at all.

Role of accountability

As is so often the case, behind each perceived supervillain stands a greater baddie lurking in the shadows and controlling the game. In education, this big bad – the father of supervillains – is high-stakes accountability.

One agent of such high-stakes accountability has been Ofsted. If there were no fear of Ofsted then we wouldn't see education myths growing up based on what we think they want to see:

- Feedback means writing individual comments in pupils' books, them responding to these comments and us responding to their response in a never-ending cycle of multicoloured pens.

- Pupils should know their target grades and how to reach them.

- Pupils need to demonstrate what they have learnt at the end of each lesson.

This final point on demonstrating learning sits at the heart of the education myths created by accountability. If we are going to be accountable for what pupils have learnt, we need to find a way to show that this learning is happening. Unfortunately, learning is invisible and happens in the heads of our pupils as they think, forget and recollect (Nuthall, 2007). It can't be seen; and yet we are called upon to show it. Once again the impossible becomes desirable.

This leads to all kinds of distortions of our teaching. We see the last 5–10 minutes of lessons being given over to 'plenaries' where pupils are expected to show what they have learnt. These range from pupils putting their hands up to show if they think they have met an objective, to the use of exit tickets where they answer a question and leave it with the teacher or write a question on a sticky note and leave it on the board as they go out (I have no idea why putting something on a sticky note is more educational. I suspect a conspiracy by the sticky note industry. It certainly seems to be a cargo-cult practice).

The end of a lesson is a terrible time to try to see what a pupil has actually learnt. You don't know if they have actually learnt something or whether they are simply mimicking what they have just heard. If it turns out they haven't learnt something – or worse, have ended up with a misconception – what are you going to do? Glance at their exit ticket and go running down the corridor to reteach it?

And yet, high-stakes accountability continues to make us teach in less effective ways in order to try to show we are effective teachers. It really is the biggest, baddest supervillain of them all.

Why do these education myths matter?

The supervillains are winning. In our schools, up and down the country, it is like the end of the second act of a Marvel movie. The education myths are driving teachers out of the classroom as they prevent us from teaching in an efficient manner and so leave workload spiralling out of control.

Myths about feedback needing individual written comments in books every couple of weeks means the conscientious teacher with ten classes is trying to mark a set of books every day – on top of everything else they need to do. If they can't keep up with this load then they are made to feel like a failure.

Myths about teaching engaging lessons with varied and memorable tasks leave teachers spending hours trying to prepare resources for ever-more elaborate lessons filled with model building, carousel tasks and competitions.

Myths about target grades leave teachers spending hours trying to find a way to make an assessment of what a pupil can do now into a prediction about what they will be able to do in several years' time – and in a way that means they can justify their data to a line manager next week.

If we don't stand up to these education myths then our world is doomed.

Learning the origin helps us to fight them

Luckily there is a ray of hope. If the movies have taught us anything, it is that to defeat our enemy, we first need to understand our enemy. By exploring the origin story of education myths, we can drag them out into the light to be exposed for what they are.

- When we see that 'minimise teacher talk' is just a hangover from the romantic meanderings of an 18th-century writer, we are better able to think again about how to make explanations more effective in our classrooms.

- When we recognise that cargo-cult practices arise when we divorce the what from the why, we can step in to stop the rot before retrieval quizzes go the way of carousel tasks.

- There is an enormous freedom that comes from realising that we can't make the impossible possible just because it is desirable. We can instead look for better ways to report on the progress our pupils are making, free from the need to gaze into the crystal ball.

- We can accept that some of the things we do are only being done out of a fear of accountability. We can then choose to be brave and put *learning* first rather than the *demonstration* of learning to outside observers.

All myths thrive in ignorance. The more we, as teachers, can learn about the simplicity of teaching well and avoiding the complications that are forced upon us, the greater the chance we have of spotting the education myths for what they are. We need to drive these villains back and save the world. Teachers, assemble!

References

Allen, R. (2018) 'What if we cannot measure pupil progress?', Becky *Allen: Musing on Education Policy* [Blog], 23 May. Retrieved from: www.bit.ly/311ihkz

Brunskill, J. and Enser, M. (2017) 'Are "knowledge organisers" now essential tools in the classroom?', *Tes* [Online], 7 April. Retrieved from: www.bit.ly/2GvBMtv

Christodoulou, D. (2014) *Seven myths about education*. Abingdon: Routledge.

Egan, K. (2002) *Getting it wrong from the beginning: our progressive inheritance from Herbert Spencer, John Dewey, and Jean Piaget*. New Haven, CT: Yale University Press.

Harvard, B. (2017) 'The pyramid of myth', *The Effortful Educator* [Blog], 29 November. Retrieved from: www.bit.ly/2KaYMyW

Karpicke, J. D. and Grimaldi, P. J. (2012) 'Retrieval-based learning: a perspective for enhancing meaningful learning', *Educational Psychology Review* 24 (3) pp. 401–418.

Nuthall, G. (2007) *The hidden lives of learners.* Wellington: NZCER.

Roediger, H. L., Putnam, A. L. and Smith, M. A. (2011) 'Ten benefits of testing and their applications to educational practice' in Mestre, J. P. and Ross, B. H. (eds) *The psychology of learning and motivation vol. 55: cognition in education.* San Diego, CA: Academic Press, pp. 1–36.

Rosenshine, B. (2012) 'Principles of instruction: research-based strategies that all teachers should know', *American Educator* 36 (1) pp. 12–19, 39. Retrieved from: www.bit.ly/2Kw17qg

Rousseau, J. (1921) *Emile, or education.* Translated by Barbara Foxley. London: Dent.

Smith, A. M., Floerke, V. A. and Thomas, A. K. (2016) 'A commentary on retrieval practice protects memory against acute stress', *Science* 354 (6315) pp. 1046–1048.

Treadaway, M. (2015) 'Why measuring pupil progress involves more than taking a straight line', *FFT Education Datalab* [Blog], 5 March. Retrieved from: www.bit.ly/2K69lDC

Worsley, P. M. (2009) '50 years ago: cargo cults of Melanesia', *Scientific American* [Online], 1 May. Retrieved from: www.bit.ly/2YsAiKP

Author bio-sketch:
Mark Enser is head of geography and research lead at Heathfield Community College. He is a regular *Tes* columnist and author of *Teach Like Nobody's Watching* and *Making Every Geography Lesson Count.*

lesson, rather than just what they will be feeling or doing. Have we planned activities that will ensure children think hard about the right things? If not, don't be surprised when children remember very little beyond the confines of that specific lesson.

Some kinds of activity we get children to do involve hard thinking, but not always about the central things we want children to understand. For example, doing practical science experiments involves lots of thinking about planning, what to do next, monitoring what is happening. In fact, the practical elements require so much mental energy that there isn't much cognitive bandwidth left over for actually thinking about the concepts that the experiment is meant to demonstrate. When Ofsted investigated science teaching in primary schools, they found that many schools mistakenly attempted to teach the concepts of science almost entirely through practical experiments:

> The misconception here is that 'working scientifically' becomes the mechanism for teaching knowledge and concepts. However, approaching the teaching of science in this way leads to a recurring problem that pupils are engaged in these lessons, but it is the experiment that is memorable and not the underlying knowledge intended to be learned. For instance, when inspectors questioned pupils during the research visits, pupils could easily recall the task carried out, but struggled to explain how the processes they were investigating actually worked. (Ofsted, 2019)

Which is not to say that children shouldn't do scientific experiments, but that teachers need to be acutely aware that pupils are highly unlikely to gain understanding of scientific concepts unless experiments are conducted after the ideas behind them have already been taught. Once the scientific concepts are secure, children are much more able to really 'think like scientists' – with the added benefit that the practical activity then consolidates understanding of the previous learning.

The same is true for activities that require children to research information for themselves. If this is done as a way of acquiring information in the first instance, then the cognitive effort of locating the correct information is unlikely to leave space for children to actually remember much about what they have found out. Children will be thinking about where they can find out what they need to and whether or not what they are reading is relevant, rather than actually thinking about what it says. If remembering what it says is important – and presumably it was or why waste time finding out about it – then teachers need to bear in mind that extra time, either before or after the research activities, will need to be spent thinking hard about it.

This problem raises its head yet again in teaching maths through problem solving. Some teachers believe that rich tasks such as investigations where children discover relationships for themselves are a much better way of teaching than telling children explicitly how to do things. Discovering is seen as more creative, more interesting, requiring more imagination and therefore much more likely to result in children really understanding the maths conceptually, rather than just regurgitating a procedure. However, while rich tasks have their place, they are completely inappropriate for the initial stage of learning, when children are encountering a concept for the first time. If we want children to become independent problem-solvers, we need to carefully and explicitly teach them so that semantic memory can begin to form. Counter-intuitive as it may seem, children do not become independent problem-solvers by independently solving problems. This is because when children are trying to solve problems before they know the necessary maths to do so, they will be expending considerable mental energy tracking what they are meant to be solving against what they have found out so far – so much so that even when they are successful, they will have forgotten what they actually did en route to finally finding the answer!

There is a lot of research that shows that teaching is much more effective when the teacher explicitly explains material in small, carefully thought-out steps, giving children lots of opportunity to practise before going onto the next small step. This is particularly true in the early knowledge acquisition phase of learning. For example, see Rosenshine (2012), Coe et al. (2014) or the 2014 Centre for Education and Statistics report *What works best: evidence-based practices to help improve NSW student performance*, all of which reach similar conclusions.

Even if we plan lessons that involve children thinking hard about the right things, and break material down into small steps, we might still have the following all-too-familiar experience. At the end of a sequence of lessons on a particular topic, a teacher feels reasonably confident that most of the class have learnt how to do whatever it was they have been studying – the grid method, for example. Children may perform reasonably well in an end-of-unit assessment. However, revisit the topic a few weeks later and not only can children not remember how to do the grid method, several deny all knowledge of having even heard of it before! This bemusing situation can leave teachers feeling rather dispirited and wondering where they have gone wrong.

Unless teachers plan opportunities to revisit concepts again – later, some time removed from recent teaching of the concept – it is likely that semantic memory

Author bio-sketch:

Clare Sealy has spent 30 years as a primary school teacher, 22 of them as head of St Matthias Primary School in Tower Hamlets in the East End of London. She has recently left headship to become of Head of Curriculum and Standards for the States of Guernsey. She blogs about how her school put educational research findings into practice at www.primarytimery. com. Her particular interests are the application of cognitive science in the classroom, rethinking assessment for learning and curriculum development. In 2018, she was named by *Tes* as one of the top ten most influential people in education.

SCREENTOPIA

BY DOUG LEMOV

At the risk of sounding like a fan-boy – and prompting the man in question to enquire about a restraining order – let me just say two things about Doug Lemov. First, I think his book *Teach like a Champion 2.0* is hands down the most practical guide to reflecting upon and improving teacher practice I've ever read. Second, my interview with Doug for my Mr Barton Maths Podcast is one of my favourite conversations with a human ever.

Now, Doug is not a maths teacher (we can't all be perfect), and yet I find his writing so applicable to my subject domain. This chapter is no exception. Here, Doug confronts the myth that technology in schools is necessarily a good thing, considering its effect on our – and our children's – ability to read. Concentrate now...

As you read this – on the Underground or in the garden, perhaps at your desk between meetings – reading as we know it is engaged in an epic battle it has all but lost.

No matter where you are, Device is there with you, cosily stowed in your pocket, chirping away pleasantly, always at your behest. Check in with a colleague or the children? Play *Candy Crush*? Find a football score? All while in line at Tesco or, better, sitting through the 10am strategy meeting? Of course, Master. It would be my pleasure. And, also, Master, please check out this video of some very adorable puppies.

Suddenly Device must always be there with you. Almost every garment you buy contains a special pocket to keep it cosy and near. Studies tell us you check it, now, 150–200 times a day. Between your browser, your email and the latest indispensable app – Hello, CalorieCounter! – you switch media sources 27 times an hour. In other words, your average duration of sustained focus on any task when Device is near is just over two minutes.

Clever Device. Once it was the servant; now it is the master.

I know, I know. You love and value reading. But you have also perhaps come to believe the myth that your lives and your children's lives – and most of all their classrooms – need more technology. They should be infused with it. It should be a seamless screentopia where we are all always connected. And that is increasingly incompatible with reading.

Consider the plight of poor Mr Dickens. Or poor Ms Morrison. Forced to compete against the shiny, the bright, the buzzing and the instantly gratifying, their endless byzantine clauses now totter sadly off, half seen, towards the distance of the page. Suddenly their very syntax is a museum piece:

> 'It was the age of foolishness, it was the epoch of belief, it was the epoch of incredulity, it was the season of Light, it was the season of Darkness, it was the spring of hope, it was the winter of despair, we had everything before us, we had nothing before us, we were all going direct to Heaven, we were all going direct the other way – in short, the period was so far like the present period, that some of its noisiest authorities insisted on its being received, for good or for evil, in the superlative degree of comparison only.'

Honestly, did you finish that sentence? Do you think your students would?

It is not just that we read less and less. It is that we read *differently*. This is the kicker, the part we all perhaps have a sense for – something Maryanne Wolf describes in technical detail in the admirably researched *Reader Come Home* (Wolf, 2018a), a book that exposes the insidiousness of the myth.

Our brains have what scientists term 'novelty bias'. Because we are predisposed to attend to new information – from an evolutionary perspective, anything new, bright and flashing could contain survival information – it gets priority over sustained focus on what we were previously thinking about.

When we read in a screened environment – on our screens or with one open around us – a cycle of expectation and gratification emerges. There is always something new and exciting and we are drawn again and again to the incoming; rewarded again and again for our distractions with a tiny surge of dopamine, until we come to expect it, to need it. As we read, this tingling for the new crowds out reflection, creative association, empathy, problem solving – the soul of deep and meaningful engagement with the ideas of a writer, speaking to us down through the centuries or from across the globe in carefully selected words.

Author bio-sketch:

Doug Lemov is the author of several books on teaching including *Teach Like a Champion* (now in it's *2.0* version) and *Reading Reconsidered*. His work at Uncommon Schools – a nonprofit organization in the US that runs high-performing schools in underserved urban communities – focuses on training teachers and is informed by video study of their daily work in the classroom.

THE DIFFERENTIATION MYTH

BY GREG ASHMAN

It is no exaggeration to say that Greg Ashman changed my life. If you listen closely to his first appearance on my podcast, you can hear my world crumbling around me as Greg challenges my long-held beliefs about teacher talk, discovery and worked examples. I've not been the same teacher since, and I'll be forever grateful.

In this chapter, Greg takes on one of the biggest myths of all – differentiation. Differentiation is the holy grail I quested after for most of my career…and never quite achieved. It was the most common feedback I received from lesson observations – 'You need to differentiate more.' It was what turned my role in the classroom into a glorified leaflet hander-outer as I strove to continually provide work to match my students' ever-changing needs. Here, Greg questions what we mean by differentiation, and whether we should strive for it at all.

You should differentiate your lessons more, right?

You can ignore the spectre in a noisy room at a busy time, but as a teacher, it is ever present, stalking you, gently tapping you on the shoulder. You dare not look around because the horrifying visage is too much to bear. 'I am already stretched as thin as linguine – perhaps even spaghetti,' you think. 'Where could I find the time to plan for yet more *differentiation*?'

I have good news. I absolve you from your years of guilt. The apparition will haunt you no longer. Differentiation as we know it is overhyped. There is very little evidence that practices that are commonly classified as aspects of differentiation make any significant difference to the quality of teaching – and there are, in some instances, good reasons to suspect that they may have a negative effect. Moreover, at its heart, the whole concept of differentiation encompasses opposite approaches, so different people could be using the same term to describe contradictory practices.

First, the bad news. Education academics and bureaucrats demand differentiation when they write regulations for teachers. For instance, the 2011 *Teachers' Standards* for schools in England state that teachers must 'know when and how to differentiate appropriately, using approaches which enable pupils to be taught effectively' (Department for Education, 2011). This is an international phenomenon, with the Australian teaching standards going further and including a scale. A graduate teacher who is just entering the profession will be expected to 'demonstrate knowledge and understanding of strategies for differentiating teaching to meet the specific learning needs of students across the full range of abilities'; whereas as an experienced 'lead', teachers will be able to 'lead colleagues to evaluate the effectiveness of learning and teaching programs differentiated for the specific learning needs of students across the full range of abilities' (Australian Institute for Teaching and School Leadership, 2011).

The regulatory enforcement of differentiation is worrying, given that I am about to cast doubt on the evidence supporting practices that sit under this term.

So, what is differentiation?

As Carol Ann Tomlinson, education professor and recognised authority on differentiation, states, 'At its most basic level, differentiation consists of the efforts of teachers to respond to variance among learners in the classroom' (Tomlinson, 2000). It is almost impossible to conceive of a teacher in an 'early years through to secondary school' setting who does not respond to variance to some extent. In my everyday teaching, I often re-explain concepts to individuals or groups of students while other students work independently. We could also reasonably argue that the process of setting or placing students into different classes within a subject based upon their prior level of performance is a form of differentiation because it is a response to variance among learners. Indeed, when I have expressed scepticism about differentiation in the past, proponents of setting have taken me to task on this basis.

However, it is clear that setting or making small adjustments to whole-class teaching are not what advocates for differentiation generally propose. To Tomlinson, differentiation is a quite specific set of strategies. It involves planning 'multiple routes for students' rather than using 'one-size-fits-all' lesson plans, as well as the use of 'small, flexible groupings' of students, materials with varying reading levels, a flexible pace and a focus on each individual student's interests and needs by giving them choice and taking account of their preferred learning styles (Tomlinson, 2005).

One part of this picture should immediately strike us as ill founded. In recent years, the notion of catering to students' learning styles has been systematically debunked by cognitive scientists and other learning experts (see e.g. 'No evidence to back idea of learning styles', 2017). Tomlinson has since responded to these efforts without entirely walking away from the concept (Tomlinson, 2010).

If we accept that learning styles lack evidence, then an interesting question arises: why would we seek to posit additional differences for which we have little evidence when there are so many *real* differences between students, particularly in their prior knowledge? My hypothesis is that differentiation, at least in part, has evolved to meet ideological needs, one of which is an exaggerated form of individualism. An individualistic educational philosophy was expressed by John Dewey in the early part of the 20th century when he wrote, 'Not knowledge or information, but self-realization, is the goal. To possess all the world of knowledge and lose one's own self is as awful a fate in education as religion' (Dewey, 1902) and 'There is … no point in the philosophy of progressive education which is sounder than its emphasis upon the importance of the participation of the learner in the formation of the purposes which direct his activities in the learning process' (Dewey, 1938). Dewey is still highly influential in university education faculties and education bureaucracies and this tradition carries through to today when advocates call for a 'student-centred' or 'learner-centred' approach to teaching and the curriculum.

Setting aside learning styles, other aspects of the Tomlinson model raise their own questions. The possible benefits of tailoring teaching more closely to each student's needs are foremost in our minds when we decide to differentiate, but what about the costs? If we arrange students in groups then we create a number of potential costs. For instance, imagine a class that runs for one hour and has the students split into six groups. If the teacher addresses the whole class then the grouping arrangement becomes pointless. If they instead decide to spend time with each group in turn then that equates to roughly ten minutes per group of direct teacher input. In addition, when the teacher is working directly with one of the groups, what will the other groups be doing? There is likely to be a need for the teacher to often break off from one group in order to redirect the students in a different group. Under such conditions, it is not entirely clear that up to 10 minutes of more tailored teaching is superior to 60 minutes of less tailored teaching.

In 1975, researchers at the University of Leicester initiated the Observational Research and Classroom Evaluation (ORACLE) project (Galton, 1987). Spurred in part by the publication in England of the Plowden Committee report into primary education, teachers had begun to move away from whole-class teaching. Many used a system of individualised instruction where teachers interacted with students individually while the rest of the class completed tasks. Some teachers made more use of group work. In each case, researchers had cause to question the value of many of the activities that took place when the teacher's attention was elsewhere.

It may be because of these practical issues that strong evidence in support of differentiation is so scarce. One promising experimental study sought to compare the effect of professional development in differentiated instruction with professional development in 'differentiated authentic assessment' along with a control group of teachers who did not receive professional development. Despite Tomlinson being one of the researchers involved in the project, they found few significant benefits of differentiated instruction versus the control (Brighton et al., 2005). The authors suggest that many schools lack the structures necessary for differentiation to be effectively developed and that differentiation requires teachers to 'dismantle their existing, persistent beliefs about teaching and learning'. So either it doesn't work in principle or it doesn't work in practice. At the very least, it seems an unlikely bet for any school seeking a professional development focus that will produce significant benefits for the learning of their students.

One approach to differentiation that has been recommended to Australian teachers by academics is known as 'Universal Design for Learning' (UDL) (Graham and Cologon, 2016). If you have grown weary of the breathless claims made for different educational programmes, you may find the UDL website (udlguidelines.cast.org) somewhat off-putting, with its images of brains with different regions shaded in various colours.

UDL offers teachers a range of principles to consider when planning lessons. There should be a range of approaches for representing knowledge to students and students should be able to demonstrate their understanding in multiple ways. By providing students with more control over their learning and a choice of activities, the hope is that they will become more engaged. A 2017 meta-analysis of research into UDL found that, although it improved the 'learning process', the effect on educational outcomes had not been demonstrated (Capp, 2017).

The lack of an effect may be due to limitations in the available research, but it may also be directly due to the application of the UDL principles. Although it may seem obvious that it is a good idea to enable students to demonstrate their understanding in multiple ways and to give them choices, these strategies could potentially cause problems.

Students do not always know the best strategy to follow. As far back as 1982, Richard Clark noted that in a number of 'aptitude-treatment interaction' studies, there was a mismatch between the learning strategies that students most enjoyed and those from which they learnt the most. Less-advanced students reported enjoying open-ended tasks, whereas they learnt more from highly structured tasks. Conversely, more-advanced students reported enjoying highly structured tasks, whereas they learnt more from open-ended tasks (Clark, 1982). Similar effects, where students prefer a method from which they learn less, have been found in a range of situations such as reading digital media versus reading print media (Singer and Alexander, 2017) and studying worked examples versus solving problems (Foster et al., 2018). Even if there are times when students make the right choices, the fact that they can make the wrong choices means that we should pause before exalting student choice as an unqualified good.

Think of it this way – who is best placed to make a decision about the next step in learning? Is it a student who does not know what she does not know and who has never been in this situation before, or is it a teacher who understands where the learning is going and who has taught students with similar profiles in the past?

Furthermore, the idea of allowing students to demonstrate understanding in multiple ways leads us directly to the contradiction at the heart of differentiation.

Imagine a student who struggles with her writing. She is a member of a science class that has conducted a number of experiments and the students are expected to present their findings in a written report. How should we differentiate to meet her needs?

One solution would be to offer her intensive writing support outside of the science class in order to improve her writing overall. Another option, directly tailored to the science lesson, may be to provide a writing frame or split the writing task down into small chunks, offering feedback at each stage. All of these strategies *address*, head-on, her difficulties with writing.

However, we might also picture an alternative. Perhaps we ask her to present her findings orally or in the form of a poster. Both of these options will involve doing a reduced volume of formal writing. Perhaps we place her in a group to construct the poster – a group where she provides the artwork and a different group member completes the writing. In this case, we are *accommodating* rather than addressing her difficulties with writing.

Accommodating is the direct opposite of addressing, and yet *all* of the options I have described could plausibly be labelled as 'differentiation'. It may sometimes be appropriate to address and it may sometimes be appropriate to accommodate, but what is the value of a term that encompasses both without distinguishing between them? Clearly, if all we ever do is accommodate a difficulty, the student will never make progress in that area of difficulty. Presumably, we would not want to do this, but we could nevertheless claim to be differentiating.

When differentiation does appear to be effective, the conditions are often different to the ones we may expect if we follow the models developed by Tomlinson or UDL. In one study, middle school science students were randomly allocated into one of two conditions. In both conditions, students listened to the same teacher presentations. However, in the control condition, students completed worksheets whereas in the differentiated condition, students completed activities of varying difficulties that were assigned to them by the teacher. They were also placed in groups so that less advanced students were assisted by more advanced partners. The researchers found some evidence of a positive effect on standardised assessments for all students for this kind of differentiation when compared with the control (Mastropieri et al., 2006).

Significantly, students had no control over their own learning in this study, with less advanced students being initially assigned the lowest level activity. They were also assigned to work with other students who could help them address their learning needs.

Although it is not experimental data, evidence from the Programme for International Student Assessment (PISA) is also suggestive of the potential value of practices commonly associated with differentiation. The Organisation for Economic Co-operation and Development (OECD) who run PISA also survey teachers about their practice and so it is possible to map the answers to various survey questions to PISA scores. In 2013, teachers were asked how often they 'give different work to the students who have difficulties learning and/or to those who can advance faster'. If you plot the average response for each country against the same country's 2012 PISA maths score, there is a slight negative correlation. In other words, in countries where teachers report more of this kind of differentiation, students do less well in maths (Ashman, 2014).

This is clearly a fairly crude level of analysis, but more sophisticated approaches tell a similar story. The OECD considers the practice of giving different work to students based upon their ability as one facet of what it defines as 'student-oriented instruction'. Other elements include assigning projects, assigning students to work on tasks in small groups and asking students to make choices about classroom activities (Echazarra et al., 2016). These are all practices associated with different forms of differentiation.

As well as teachers, PISA also asks students about the practices they encounter in their lessons and Caro et al. (2016) were able to examine the correlation between these survey responses and maths scores for the 2012 PISA round of assessment (maths was a focus area of PISA 2012). They were able to look at the relationship for data within a participating country. Across the 62 education systems they analysed, there was a consistently negative relationship between student-oriented instruction, as reported by students, and PISA maths score. The more of these practices that were present, the lower the maths performance.

As with all correlational data, it cannot be used to prove that student-oriented instruction *caused* lower maths scores. There could be some other factor involved. For instance, it is plausible that in classrooms where behaviour is poor, teachers make more use of these strategies and it is actually the poor behaviour that leads to lower maths scores. However, such a trend is highly suggestive. If differentiation were the panacea that it is often presented as being, we would expect to find a positive association.

So there is clearly something spectral about differentiation. Stare too hard and it fades away. Try to reason with it and you encounter its internal contradictions. Should you accommodate students' needs or address them? The spectre cannot say. Instead, we need a more specific language to describe how to deal with the variance between different students. Instead of one, mushy and vague term that acts as a barrier to communication, we need clearer and more specific ones that generate testable predictions.

Is differentiation a myth? It depends what you mean by *differentiation*. And that's the problem.

References

Ashman, G. (2014) 'TALIS data on differentiation', *Filling the Pail* [Blog], 5 July. Retrieved from: www.bit.ly/32ZjNVT

Australian Institute for Teaching and School Leadership (2011) *Australian professional standards for teachers.* Melbourne: Education Council. Retrieved from: www.bit.ly/331yxUs

Brighton, C. M., Hertberg, H. L., Moon, T R., Tomlinson, C. A. and Callahan, C. M. (2005) *The feasibility of high-end learning in a diverse middle school.* Storrs, CT: University of Connecticut National Research Center on the Gifted and Talented.

Capp, M. J. (2017) 'The effectiveness of universal design for learning: a meta-analysis of literature between 2013 and 2016', *International Journal of Inclusive Education*, 21 (8) pp. 791–807.

Caro, D. H., Lenkeit, J. and Kyriakides, L. (2016) 'Teaching strategies and differential effectiveness across learning contexts: evidence from PISA 2012', *Studies in Educational Evaluation* 49 (1) pp. 30–41.

Clark, R. E. (1982) 'Antagonism between achievement and enjoyment in ATI studies', *Educational Psychologist* 17 (2) pp. 92–101.

Department for Education (2011) *Teachers' standards: guidance for school leaders, school staff and governing bodies.* London: The Stationery Office. Retrieved from: www.bit.ly/2YrExSY

Dewey, J. (1902) *The child and the curriculum.* Chicago, IL: The University of Chicago Press.

Dewey, J. (1938) *Experience and education.* New York, NY: Kappa Delta Pi.

Echazarra, A., Salinas, D., Méndez, I., Denis, V. and Rech, G. (2016) *How teachers teach and student learn: successful strategies for school.* OECD education working paper 130. Paris: OECD Directorate for Education and Skills.

Foster, N. L., Rawson, K. A. and Dunlosky, J. (2018) 'Self-regulated learning of principle-based concepts: do students prefer worked examples, faded examples, or problem solving?', *Learning and Instruction* 55 (1) pp. 124–138.

Galton, M. (1987) 'An ORACLE chronicle: a decade of classroom research', *Teaching and Teacher Education* 3 (4) pp. 299–313.

Graham, L. J. and Cologon, K. (2016) 'Explainer: what is differentiation and why is it poorly understood?', *The Conversation* [Website], 8 March. Retrieved from: www.bit.ly/2GAQSya

Mastropieri, M. A., Scruggs, T. E., Norland, J. J., Berkeley, S., McDuffie, K., Tornquist, E. H. and Connors, N. (2006) 'Differentiated curriculum enhancement in inclusive middle school science: effects on classroom and high-stakes tests', *Journal of Special Education* 40 (3) pp. 130–137.

'No evidence to back idea of learning styles' [Letter to the editor] (2017) *The Guardian* [Online], 12 March. Retrieved from: www.bit.ly/2Mw31I6

Singer, L. M. and Alexander, P. A. (2017) 'Reading across mediums: effects of reading digital and print texts on comprehension and calibration', *Journal of Experimental Education* 85 (1) pp. 155–172.

Tomlinson, C. A. (2000) *Differentiation of instruction in the elementary grades.* Reston, VA: ERIC Digest. Retrieved from: www.bit.ly/2ZkNFdb

Tomlinson, C. A. (2005) 'Traveling the road to differentiation in staff development', *Journal of Staff Development* 26 (4) pp. 8–12.

Tomlinson, C. A. (2010) 'Carol Ann Tomlinson on learning styles', *ASCD Inservice* [Blog], 15 June. Retrieved from: www.bit.ly/32YD7CP

Author bio-sketch:

Greg Ashman is a teacher and head of research at Ballarat Clarendon College, Victoria. He is a prolific blogger and has recently written a book, *The Truth about Teaching: an evidence-informed guide for new teachers.* Prior to moving to Australia, Greg worked at a number of comprehensive schools in London.

THE MYTH THAT BLOCKING ONE'S STUDY OR PRACTICE BY TOPIC OR SKILL ENHANCES LEARNING

BY ROBERT AND ELIZABETH BJORK

It's hard to know where to begin with the Bjorks. In his foreword to the US version of my book, Dylan Wiliam describes Robert Bjork as 'the world's leading expert in memory', and yet as a teacher – and therefore someone very much in the memory business – I remained ignorant of the Bjorks' work for 12 years. Robert and Elizabeth's appearance on my podcast was a game changer for me in terms of my thinking about what may well be the ultimate education myth – that learning and performance are the same thing. Moreover, that learning actually benefits from high classroom performance (and the conditions that lead to it). The 10,000+ downloads the podcast has currently attracted suggests it was seminal for other listeners too.

It is the Bjorks' focus on what they term 'desirable difficulties' that has most significantly changed my day-to-day classroom practice. Trying to move away from the cosy, comforting conditions that inspire high performance but low learning was a challenge – for both me and my students – for the simple reason that it feels tough. Testing replaced repeated study; interleaved practice replaced massed practice; and retrieval of knowledge now takes place over time instead of in nice, tidy blocks. Those last two desirable difficulties are the focus of this chapter, and they have profound implications for all teachers and students.

As learners, we are often admonished – starting at an early age – to 'focus on one thing at a time', to 'finish what you started', and so forth. We are urged to be 'focused', not 'flighty' or 'scatterbrained'. Such advice seems like good advice, not only as to how we should manage our own efforts to learn, but also how we, as teachers or parents, should manage the instruction of our students or children.

But is such advice good advice? We do know, of course, that individuals can suffer from attention deficit disorder, an inability to stay focused on the task or subject at hand, but that is a different issue from whether one should block or interleave the study or practice of the components of to-be-learned knowledge or skills. In fact, a growing body of research suggests that interleaving, not blocking, enhances the learning and transfer of to-be-learned skills and knowledge. In this chapter, we first discuss the evidence that interleaved practice can enhance the learning and transfer of perceptual-motor skills. We then discuss the benefits of interleaving in the domain of verbal/conceptual skills; and we conclude with a brief discussion of theoretical conjectures as to why interleaving can foster long-term retention and transfer of knowledge and skills.

Interleaved versus blocked practice in the learning of perceptual-motor skills

Research on interleaved versus blocked practice of motor skills traces back to a critical study carried out 40 years ago by two kinesiology graduate students (Shea and Morgan, 1979) at the University of Colorado. Shea and Morgan built an apparatus that would let them test the speed and accuracy of participants' ability to release a start button, grab a tennis ball from a slot in the apparatus, knock over three of six hinged barriers in a prescribed order, and then place the tennis ball in a prescribed slot, thereby stopping the timer. There were three such movement patterns to be learned and all participants received 54 practice trials, 18 on each to-be-learned sequence; but those trials were blocked by pattern for half of the participants and interleaved randomly for the other participants.

During the learning phase, blocked practice appeared to be clearly more effective than interleaved practice: both groups improved across the practice trials, but the participants given blocked practice were able to knock the barriers over in the prescribed pattern more rapidly throughout the practice phase than were the participants given random practice. On a retention test administered 10 days later, however, and whether it was administered under blocked or random/interleaved conditions, the results were very different. When the retention test was administered under interleaved conditions, the blocked-practice group performed far worse than did the interleaved-practice group; and when the retention test was administered under blocked conditions, the difference between the groups was very small, but even then the direction of the difference favoured the interleaved-practice group.

Across the intervening years, there have been many replications of the benefits of interleaved over blocked practice for different skills (for a review,

what helped them learn the artists' styles better, blocking or interleaving – were told that 90% of participants in the paintings task are better at identifying new paintings by the interleaved artists than they are at identifying new paintings by the blocked artists. After getting that message, 60% of the participants still said that blocking was as good or better than interleaving. Participants in another condition were told not only that most people do better with interleaving, but also (a) why the sense that blocking helps one see the defining characteristics of a given artist's paintings is misleading and (b) why interleaving helps seeing the differences between artists, which is a 'crucial' factor in learning the artists' styles. Even then, only about half the participants said that interleaving helped them learn the artists' styles. When participants were given feedback as to their actual performance ('You got X/24 of the blocked artists correct, and you got Y/24 of the interleaved artists correct. You did better on the [blocked/ interleaved] artists') and then asked to say why by selecting between (a) 'That particular set of artists was easier to learn' and (b) 'That schedule is more effective', 58% of the 45 participants who did better on the interleaved artists said that those artists were easier to learn, whereas 80% of the 20 participants who did better on the blocked artists said that the blocked schedule was more effective. Finally, when participants were asked to say what schedule they would use in teaching students if they were an art teacher, twice as many participants (50 versus 25) said a blocked schedule as said an interleaved schedule.

So why do most participants think that blocking the exemplars of a given category enhances inductive learning? One factor, alluded to already, is that blocking creates a sense of fluency with respect to noticing the similarities across a given artist's paintings, whereas interleaving creates a sense of confusion and difficulty in noticing those similarities. Another factor is that participants are likely to come to the experiment with a belief that blocking is good – because blocking is so commonly used in real-world settings, including by the participants' teachers. That participants come to such an experiment with the belief that blocking, not interleaving, fosters inductive learning is supported by the results of an experiment by Tauber et al. (2012). In this experiment the participants were tasked with learning the characteristics of eight families of birds (warblers, finches, etc.) and were shown pictures of members of these families, one bird at a time. After a picture was shown, they saw a message, such as 'You have just studied a jay. Click on the bird family that you would like to see next.' Overwhelmingly, participants chose to see another picture in the same family – that is, another picture of a jay in this example.

The benefits of spacing/interleaving have been shown in the inductive learning of other categories as well, such as species of butterflies (Birnbaum et al., 2013);

and how such benefits are modulated or eliminated by various manipulations has been explored (see e.g. Kang and Pashler, 2012; Wahlheim et al., 2011). In a potentially important new context – foreign-language learning – Pan et al. (in press) found that the learning of Spanish-language verb conjugations profits from interleaving.

To conclude this section it is important to mention that Rothkopf – in saying that spacing is the enemy of induction – was not entirely wrong. In fact, in their discussion, Kornell and Bjork (2008) asserted – notwithstanding the benefits of interleaving they found in the inductive learning of painters' styles – 'There surely are situations in which massing is more effective for induction than is spacing' (p. 590), and they report an experiment designed to illustrate the point. Participants had to figure out and remember for a later test the single word that could fill in the blanks before a set of other words, such as '_____ cracker, _____ wood, _____ side, _____ ant, _____ truck, _____ arm', where the answer in this case is *fire*. Spacing/interleaving of such materials made it extremely difficult to solve such problems and massing, not spacing, led to better end-of-experiment recall of the words that solved the 12 such problems. Kornell and Bjork concluded by saying 'whether spacing is the friend or enemy of induction is a matter for sophisticated theorizing, because induction is a product of conceptual and memory processes that are open to multiple situational influences', but 'that in less contrived and more complex real-world learning situations, spacing appears to facilitate induction' (p. 591).

Such conceptual and memory processes have been explored by Carvalho and Goldstone (2014; 2015) in a systematic programme of experiments, most requiring participants to learn categories of 'blobs' based on identifying perceptual features of such shapes that distinguished one category of blobs from another category. Across that programme of research, Carvalho and Goldstone have demonstrated that when the biggest challenge confronting learners is to identify the feature(s) that define a category (versus distinguishing between categories), blocking – not interleaving – tends to enhance such inductive learning. That conclusion bears on the question taken up in the next section of this chapter, namely, why and when – from a theoretical standpoint – does interleaving support long-term retention and transfer?

Why does interleaving support the long-term retention and transfer of knowledge and skills?

In the domain of learning motor skills, the idea that the 'contextual interference' caused by interleaving to-be-learned skills – while depressing momentary performance – sets the stage for enhanced learning (Battig, 1979) has been very prominent, especially after Shea and Morgan (1979), motivated by Battig's ideas, provided the demonstration experiment discussed earlier in this chapter. As embellished by Shea and Morgan and by Shea and Zimny (1983) in their 'elaboration and distinctiveness hypothesis', the benefits of interleaving result from the contrasts and comparisons that are evoked during an interleaved schedule, but not (or at least to a much lesser extent) during a blocked schedule. Such contrasts and comparisons then lead to more elaborative and distinctive processing, which, in turn, enhances long-term retention and transfer.

An alternative interpretation is the 'forgetting and reconstruction hypothesis' or 'reloading hypothesis' (Lee and Magill, 1983; 1985). The basic idea behind this hypothesis is that during blocked practice, forgetting or interference between trials is minimal; whereas with interleaved practice, the switching between or among the to-be-executed skills requires a reloading of the to-be-executed motor programme, thereby providing more effective practice for a post-training test of retention or transfer. Cuddy and Jacoby (1982) argued for, and provided evidence for, much the same idea in the domain of verbal learning. For an excellent review of contextual interference effects and interpretations, see Lee (2012).

In the domain of learning mathematical concepts and procedures, Rohrer and colleagues (e.g. Rohrer et al., 2019) have argued for – and provided convincing evidence for – the idea that interleaving enhances a learner's ability to select the appropriate procedure when confronted with a problem to solve on a post-instruction test of retention or transfer. Thus, for example, a mathematics workbook that presents a series of problems all to be solved via the Pythagorean theorem provides students with a kind of crutch, in effect, telling them what procedure to draw on to solve any one of the presented problems. On some later post-instruction test that really matters, however, no such crutch will be provided. That is, different types of problems will typically be presented in a more or less random order on such tests and the procedure to use in solving each of them will not be specified. In other words, while interleaved instruction and practice exercises processes that will be crucial for achieving good performance on post-instruction tests of retention and transfer, blocked practice does not.

Finally, in the domain of learning concepts and categories, there is evidence – alluded to earlier – that interleaving can draw attention to and enhance the encoding of features that distinguish between the exemplars of different categories and concepts.

Concluding comments

In the context of real-world education, the potential of interleaving to enhance the effectiveness of instruction and self-regulated learning seems very substantial, even exciting. Much of its relevance to real-world education still needs to be determined, however, such as the chunk size (so to speak) of the materials to be interleaved and the extent to which the interleaved materials should or should not be related and potentially confusable. And then there is the biggest hurdle of all: convincing students and teachers that interleaving is good for them, despite the facts that it poses difficulties, often leads to worse performance during instruction than does blocked practice, and differs from what students, teachers, and parents have experienced in the past. It is in that domain that the audiences for this book – teachers, students, and parents – have an important role to play.

Bibliography

Battig, W. F. (1979) 'The flexibility of human memory' in Cermak, L. S. and Craik, F. I. M. (eds) *Levels of processing in human memory.* Hillsdale, NJ: Erlbaum, pp. 23–44.

Birnbaum, M. S., Kornell, N., Bjork, E. L. and Bjork, R. A. (2013) 'Why interleaving enhances inductive learning: the roles of discrimination and retrieval', *Memory & Cognition* 41 (3) pp. 392–402.

Carlson, R. A. and Yaure, R. G. (1990) 'Practice schedules and the use of component skills in problem solving', *Journal of Experimental Psychology: Learning, Memory, and Cognition* 16 (3) pp. 484–496.

Carvalho, P. F. and Goldstone, R. L. (2014) 'Putting category learning in order: category structure and temporal arrangement affect the benefit of interleaved over blocked study', *Memory & Cognition* 42 (3) pp. 481–495.

Carvalho, P. F. and Goldstone, R. L. (2015) 'The benefits of interleaved and blocked study: different tasks benefit from different schedules of study', *Psychonomic Bulletin & Review* 22 (1) pp. 281–285.

Cuddy, L. J. and Jacoby, L. L. (1982) 'When forgetting helps memory: an analysis of repetition effects', *Journal of Verbal Learning and Verbal Behavior* 21 (4) pp. 451–467.

Goode, S. and Magill, R. A. (1986) 'Contextual interference effects in learning three badminton serves', *Research Quarterly for Exercise and Sport* 57 (4) pp. 308–314.

Hall, K. G., Domingues, D. A. and Cavazos, R. (1994) 'Contextual interference effects with skilled baseball players', *Perceptual and Motor Skills* 78 (3) pp. 835–841.

Jamieson, B. A. and Rogers, W. A. (2000) 'Age-related effects of blocked and random practice schedules on learning a new technology', *Journal of Gerontology: Psychological Sciences* 55 (6) pp. 343–353.

Kang, S. H. K. and Pashler, H. (2012) 'Learning painting styles: spacing is advantageous when it promotes discriminative contrast', *Applied Cognitive Psychology* 26 (1) pp. 97–103.

Kornell, N. and Bjork, R. A. (2008) 'Learning concepts and categories: is spacing the "enemy of induction"?', *Psychological Science* 19 (6) 585–592.

Kornell, N., Castel, A. D., Eich, T. S. and Bjork, R. A. (2010) 'Spacing as the friend of both memory and induction in younger and older adults', *Psychology and Aging* 25 (2) pp. 498–503.

Lee, T. D. (2012) 'Contextual interference: generalizability and limitations' in Hodges, N. J. and Williams, A. M. (eds) *Skill acquisition in sport: research, theory and practice*. London: Routledge, pp. 79–93.

Lee, T. D. and Magill, R. A. (1983) 'The locus of contextual interference in motor-skill acquisition', *Journal of Experimental Psychology: Learning, Memory, and Cognition* 9 (4) pp. 730–746.

Lee, T. D. and Magill, R. A. (1985) 'Can forgetting facilitate skill acquisition?' in Goodman, D., Wilberg, R. B. and Franks, I. M. (eds) *Differing perspectives in motor learning, memory, and control*. Amsterdam: Elsevier, pp. 3–22.

Lin, C. H., Winstein, C. J., Fisher, B. E. and Wu, A. D. (2010a) 'Neural correlates of the contextual interference effect in motor learning: a transcranial magnetic stimulation investigation', *Journal of Motor Behavior* 42 (4) pp. 223–232.

Lin, C. H., Wu, A. D., Udompholkul, P. and Knowlton, B. J. (2010b) 'Contextual interference effects in sequence learning for young and older adults', *Psychology and Aging* 25 (4) pp. 929–939.

Pan, S. C., Tajran, J., Lovelett, J., Osuna, J. and Rickard, T. C (in press) 'Does interleaved practice enhance foreign language learning?', *Journal of Educational Psychology*.

Rickard, T. C., Lau, J. S. and Pashler, H. (2008) 'Spacing and the transition from calculation to retrieval', *Psychonomic Bulletin & Review* 15 (3) pp. 656-661.

Rohrer, D. and Taylor, K. (2007) 'The shuffling of mathematics practice problems improves learning', *Instructional Science* 35 (6) pp. 481–498.

Rohrer, D., Dedrick, R. F. and Burgess, K. (2014) 'The benefit of interleaved mathematics practice is not limited to superficially similar kinds of problems', *Psychonomic Bulletin & Review* 21 (5) pp. 1323–1330.

Rohrer, D., Dedrick, R. F., Hartwig, M. K. and Cheung, C. (2019) 'A randomized controlled trial of interleaved mathematics practice', *Journal of Educational Psychology*. Advance online publication.

Rohrer, D., Dedrick, R. F. and Stershic, S. (2015) 'Interleaved practice improves mathematics learning', *Journal of Educational Psychology* 107 (3) pp. 900–908.

Sana, F., Yan, V. X. and Kim, J. A. (2017) 'Study sequence matters for the inductive learning of cognitive concepts', *Journal of Educational Psychology* 109 (1) pp. 84–98.

Shea, J. B. and Morgan, R. L. (1979) 'CI effects on the acquisition, retention, and transfer of a motor skill', *Journal of Experimental Psychology: Human Learning and Memory* 5 (2) pp. 179–187.

Shea, J. B. and Zimny, S. T. (1983) 'Context effects in memory and learning movement information' in Magill, R. A. (ed.) *Memory and control of action*. Amsterdam: Elsevier, pp. 345–366.

Simon, D. A. and Bjork, R. A. (2001) 'Metacognition in motor learning', *Journal of Experimental Psychology: Learning, Memory, and Cognition* 27 (4) pp. 907–912.

Soderstrom, N. C. and Bjork, R. A. (2015) 'Learning versus performance: an integrative review', *Perspectives on Psychological Science* 10 (2) pp. 176–199.

Ste-Marie, D. M., Clark, S. E., Findlay, L. C. and Latimer, A. E. (2004) 'High levels of contextual interference enhance handwriting skill acquisition', *Journal of Motor Behavior* 36 (1) pp. 115–126.

Tauber, S. K., Dunlosky, J., Rawson, K. A., Wahlheim, C. N. and Jacoby, L. L. (2013) 'Self-regulated learning of a natural category: do people interleave or block exemplars during study?', *Psychonomic Bulletin & Review* 20 (2) pp. 356–363.

Taylor, K. and Rohrer, D. (2010) 'The effects of interleaved practice', *Applied Cognitive Psychology* 24 (6) pp. 837–848.

Vlach, H. A. and Sandhofer, C. M. (2012) 'Distributing learning over time: the spacing effect in children's acquisition and generalization of science concepts', *Child Development* 83 (4) pp. 1137–1144.

Vlach, H. A., Sandhofer, C. M. and Kornell, N. (2008) 'The spacing effect in children's memory and category induction', *Cognition* 109 (1) pp. 163–167.

Wahlheim, C. N., Dunlosky, J. and Jacoby, L. L. (2011) 'Spacing enhances the learning of natural concepts: an investigation of mechanisms, metacognition, and aging', *Memory & Cognition* 39 (5) 750–763.

Yan, V. X., Bjork, E. L. and Bjork, R. A. (2016) 'On the difficulty of mending metacognitive illusions: a priori theories, fluency effects, and misattributions of the interleaving benefit', *Journal of Experimental Psychology: General* 145 (7) pp. 918–933.

Yan, V. X., Soderstrom, N.C., Seneviratna, G. S., Bjork, E. L and Bjork, R. A. (2017) 'How should exemplars be sequenced in inductive learning? Empirical evidence versus learners' opinions', *Journal of Experimental Psychology: Applied* 23 (4) pp. 403–416.

Author bio-sketch:

Dr Elizabeth Ligon Bjork is Professor and Past Senior Vice Chair in the Department of Psychology at the University of California, Los Angeles, where she has also chaired UCLA's Academic Senate, received UCLA's Distinguished Teaching Award, and held leadership positions in efforts to enhance undergraduate education, including the training of teaching assistants, redesigning the campus-wide GE programme, awarding Instructional Improvement Grants, and guiding the Undergraduate Student Initiated Education (USIE) programme. Main themes of her research are the role of inhibitory processes in creating an adaptive memory system and how principles of learning discovered in the laboratory can be applied to enhance instructional practices and self-directed learning. She is a Fellow of the Society of Experimental Psychologists, a Fellow of the Association for Psychological Science, and has served on the editorial boards of several journals and on review panels for NIMH and NSF. Most recently, she was a joint recipient with Robert Bjork, of the James McKeen Cattell Fellow Award, recognizing outstanding contributions to psychological research addressing a critical problem in society.

Dr Robert A. Bjork is Distinguished Research Professor in the Department of Psychology at the University of California, Los Angeles. His research focuses on the interrelationships of forgetting, remembering, and learning in the functional architecture of how humans learn and remember, and on the implications of the science of learning for instruction, practice, and training. He has served as president or chair of multiple scientific organizations, including the Association for Psychological Science, and he is the recipient of multiple awards and honours, including UCLA's Distinguished Teaching Award and the American Psychological Association's Distinguished Service to Psychological Science Award. He is a Fellow of the American Academy of Arts and Sciences.

TEACHER-LED INSTRUCTION AND STUDENT-CENTRED LEARNING ARE OPPOSITES

BY TOM SHERRINGTON

▬

Tom Sherrington is the author of one of my favourite education books of all time – *The Learning Rainforest*. In it he presents a structure that schools, leadership teams, departments and individual teachers can adopt to get the most out of their students in terms of enjoyment and understanding of their subject.

In that book, Tom is very careful to avoid saying 'This is wrong, and this is right.' Clearly student learning is more subtle than that. And yet, over the past few years, particularly on Twitter, there has grown a real divide between educators proposing one form of classroom experience versus another. In this chapter, Tom addresses that divide head-on, arguing that it is indeed a myth – and a potentially harmful one at that.

Is it a myth or a straw man?

I think this is an important question to ask at the outset. There's not much value in making a case for a set of ideas representing a myth if hardly anyone holds those views. But what level of evidence is needed to support the assertion that something is a myth? Does it have to be a widely held set of ideas? Do a few examples provide enough proof? It seems to me that we could expend a lot of energy seeking to prove that something is a myth rather than exploring the more interesting and important ideas that emerge from examining the myth itself.

For this chapter, I am simply going to satisfy myself – and hopefully the majority of readers – that, based on my experience of engaging with the education world, this myth is real enough, reasonably common and is, therefore, worthy of exploration:

Teacher-led instruction and student-centred learning are opposites; they are in opposition. This has implications for the way teachers teach and the way they enact the curriculum.

It's also my view that there are plenty of people on both sides of this opposition; it's not all coming from one side. Examples are easy to find. Exhibit A – perhaps the purest expression of the myth I have found – is a poster produced by a US company called Epiphany Learning (2016). Their evangelism is embedded in the 'epiphany' branding; these are not just ideas to share – they represent some kind of revelation; an awakening. The poster I have in mind is readily available online. It sets out the difference between observations of teacher-led and student-led learning environments. On the teacher-led side, we have the subheading: 'Command & Control'. On the student-led side we have: 'Engage & Empower'. Already, this is the myth writ large and their standpoint is clear. This is then followed by a set of opposing descriptions such as:

Teacher-led	Student-led
Classrooms are quiet and controlled	Classrooms may appear busy and chaotic
Teacher are responsible for what students need	Learners are self-aware and can advocate for their own needs
Teachers focus on subject level content	Teachers lead, coach and inspire learners to find passion on subject matter
Failure is perceived as bad	Failure is recognised as a powerful teaching moment
Learning is shallow and memorised	Learning is deep and passionate.

In this poster, the opposition is explicit; unequivocal. And utterly ludicrous.

I don't know about you, but if you've ever worked in a regular comprehensive school and you want students to learn something really well, 'quiet and controlled' sounds pretty good! And yes, I am largely responsible for what students need. That's my job. And, of course, as someone who believes that my subjects (physics, science, maths) have inherent value, I'm not going to accept for a second that my passionate teacher-led instruction is anything less than straight-up awe-inspiring and secures deep learning that students will remember.

Of course, this poster is an extreme case bordering on self-parody. But it's not the only example by a long way; student-centred 'engage and empower' language crops up all the time. A quick browse through the output of Edutopia. com would reinforce the view that this side of the myth is prevalent.

On the other side, it is not difficult to find strong advocates of teacher-led instruction as a superior form of teaching to student-led processes that are variously called discovery learning, problem-based learning, project-based learning and inquiry learning. Different people will be at pains to define these things as distinct modes of learning where others will lump them all together. Some opponents of student-centred approaches are so absolute in their position, they appear not to be able to countenance the notion that students can reasonably be said to lead their learning at all. In this case, I don't have one neat example but I would argue that it's reasonably common to encounter arguments made in blogs and on social media such as:

- 'Students don't know enough about the curriculum to make good choices about what to learn.'

- 'Inquiry learning and problem-based learning should have no place in the curriculum because direct instruction will always work better so the opportunity cost can't be justified.'

- 'Student agency is not necessary or relevant in the classroom.'

- 'Group work, projects and forms of discovery learning are inherently low level and/or ineffective and lead to low standards.'

So, on the surface at least, I'd say that this myth is certainly 'out there'. But why is it a myth? My contention is that the opposition is largely misplaced, with the true level of disagreement exaggerated by poorly defined concepts and de-contextualised generalisations. In reality, in a school curriculum that is rich and broad, leading to deep learning, both teacher-led learning and student-centeredness will be woven together; blended and sequenced; integrated in a proportionate manner.

I'll address this through three different lines of argument.

1. The 'Minimally guided instruction' debate.

Aspects of this discussion are played out in a fascinating manner in the publication of and responses to the famous 2006 paper by Kirschner et al., 'Why minimal guidance during instruction does not work'. For some people, this paper represents the cornerstone for their staunch support for teacher-led instruction.

In their conclusion, Kirschner et al. suggest that:

> In so far as there is any evidence from controlled studies, it almost uniformly supports direct, strong instructional guidance rather than constructivist-based minimal guidance during the instruction of novice to intermediate learners. Even for students with considerable prior

knowledge, strong guidance while learning is most often found to be equally effective as un-guided approaches. Not only is unguided instruction normally less effective; there is also evidence that it may have negative results when students acquire misconceptions or incomplete or disorganized knowledge.

However, in their 2007 response to this paper, Hmelo-Silver et al. argue that Kirschner et al. have wrongly blurred the lines between discovery learning and the more structured approaches of problem-based learning (PBL) and inquiry learning (IL). They argue that: 'It is clear that the claim that PBL and IL "does not work" is not well supported, and, in fact, there is support for the alternative.'

As a non-expert in the field of education research – along with most teachers – it can be confusing and frustrating to be presented with opposing cases that include catch-all statements like 'It is clear that...' or 'The evidence almost uniformly supports...' as if both sets of researchers are claiming victory in a right-wrong debate. I have met a teacher who argues that Kirschner et al. 'demolish discovery learning' and another very recently who suggested the Hmelo-Silver paper represents a 'total takedown of the ludicrous Kirschner paper'. Surely both of these people can't be right?

However, on closer reading, the arguments are much more subtle. Kirschner et al. present their case most strongly for novice and intermediate learners but they appear to concede that for students approaching a more expert position, the different approaches are at least 'equally effective', which means the debate is more about sequencing approaches appropriately in the learning journey – students will reach a point where these approaches represent a genuine choice. Hmelo-Silver et al. seem to agree:

> We would argue that 'Does it work?' is the wrong question. The more important questions to ask are under what circumstances do these guided inquiry approaches work, what are the kinds of outcomes for which they are effective, what kinds of valued practices do they promote, and what kinds of support and scaffolding are needed for different populations and learning goals?

They suggest that, rather than a crude advocacy for IL and PBL as effective strategies, a different line of reasoning is needed:

> While we are not arguing against various forms of direct and more heavily guided instruction, of the sort that Kirschner et al. advocate, it is still unclear how to balance IL and PBL (which are more constructivist and experiential) with direct instructional guidance. We believe that

more directed guidance needs to build on student thinking. As a field we need to develop deeper and more detailed understandings of the interrelationships between the various instructional approaches and their impact on learning outcomes in different contexts.

Here is a welcome acknowledgement of a grey area; a lack of clarity and the need for more detailed understanding. Hmelo-Silver et al. are not actually supporting the myth of opposition; it's a more that they are protesting at the mischaracterisation of student-centred approaches as being 'minimally guided' and are at pains to stress the extent to which teacher instruction plays a role. Seizing this as an opportunity to reinforce their argument and its basis in cognitive load theory, in a response to the response, Sweller et al. (2007) argue the following:

> In many ways, both Schmidt et al. (2007) and Hmelo-Silver et al. (2007) support our argument that direct instructional guidance is of the ultimate importance. Both papers stress that modern PBL/IL are very structured with strong scaffolding and as we understand their argument, that the more structured they are, the better they work. If there is a disagreement, it is that both commentaries stop short of what we see as the ultimate conclusion, namely, a need for the major instructional emphasis to be on direct, explicit instruction such as worked examples, case studies as modeling examples, or just tuition. Weak guidance forces learners to rely on weak problem-solving strategies and for at least two decades, weak problem-solving strategies have been known to impose a heavy, extraneous cognitive load.

My take on this, taking the research debate and referencing my own experience, is that we would most certainly be unwise to downgrade teacher-led instruction. It is the bedrock of ensuring that learning happens successfully. However, that does not mean that we can't conceive of more expansive long-term processes such that teacher-led instruction is part and parcel of a wider approach; an approach where, over time, students begin learning in problem-based contexts or use the knowledge they acquire to pursue a form of inquiry.

2. Successful learning is inherently student-centred even if teacher-led

After reading and distilling the key findings from the research cited in Graham Nuthall's *Hidden Lives of Learners* (2007), Dan Willingham's *Why Don't Students Like School?* (2009), Dylan Wiliam's Embedding *Formative Assessment* (2011), Barak Rosenshine's 'Principles of Instruction' (2012) or Arthur Shimamura's *MARGE* (2018), I would argue that teacher-led instruction cannot reasonably be framed in opposition to student-centred learning because successful learning is always inherently student-centred. Teachers cannot be said to have undertaken successful instruction unless their students, as individuals, have secured successful learning – and this requires their active involvement, their mental engagement, their conscious effort and active schema-building.

Let me give some specific examples:

- Both Wiliam (2011) in his ideas about responsive teaching and Rosenshine (2012), with his strong emphasis on checking for understanding, suggest that, in order to conduct effective instructional interactions, the teaching needs to be highly interactive. In order to plan the next steps in the process, teachers need feedback from their students that indicates the level of confidence, fluency and accuracy that individuals are developing. Essentially, effective instruction depends on teachers being guided by their students' responses; they will adapt, adjust, push on, re-teach, provide more supports, take scaffolds away, give more or less feedback, follow different lines of reasoning – all driven by the students. How can we ensure our students are forming secure schema for the ideas in hand if we do not engage them in processes that reveal how their learning is progressing? To me, this is what student-centredness is about: it puts the emphasis on the learning that is taking place, not the activities or tasks teachers are engaging in.

- In the five strategies for effective formative assessment developed by Wiliam and colleagues (explored in Wiliam, 2011), two of them explicitly place students at the centre of the process:

  - Activate students as owners of their learning.

  - Activate students are resources for each other.

Not only is it more time efficient for teachers to harness students to check the quality or accuracy of their own responses – magnifying the frequency and quantity of feedback they receive – it can also lead to a much stronger impact on outcomes. If students generate their own feedback, comparing their work to exemplars or seeing correct solutions, they can often internalise and respond to the feedback more successfully than with teacher-generated feedback. In this context, responsive teaching that generates effective feedback is likely to be highly student-centred in the approaches used.

- It's been identified in various broad analyses of learning approaches – including by John Hattie (2009) and the Education Endowment Foundation (2018) – that metacognitive strategies have a strong relative effect, suggesting that metacognition plays an important role in successful learning. Nuthall (2007) describes how students engage in self-talk, narrating their thinking, with important positive effects. Whilst teachers play an important role in modelling these metacognitive strategies, ultimately, students must learn to use them themselves. This extends to the wider notion of self-regulation, where students plan, monitor and evaluate their progress through a given task. This can only be enacted by students themselves; therefore, where instruction has been successful, it can only be so if teachers have succeeded in developing students' capacity to lead their own learning at various levels, from problem-solving to longer-term task completion. Students have to make sense of any set of ideas for themselves; they have to write, speak and perform themselves; they have to form successful study habits and pass exams themselves. Unless teachers are consciously fostering these strongly student-centred elements of the learning process – sometimes referred to as independent learning – they're much less likely to happen.

The myth is that these student-centred elements of successful learning can be fostered without being teacher-led; that they somehow come into being. However, whilst some students might develop these characteristics more independently, our goal as teachers is for everyone to succeed and we cannot simply leave this to chance. Supporting students to be successful as independent learners is part and parcel of instructional teaching. They are not opposites; they're actually inseparable.

I find Clark et al.'s *American Educator* article (2012) incredibly helpful in this area as they explain the confusion over the meaning and implications of 'constructivism'. Citing Mayer, they suggest that people have confused the sound theory of constructivism, which asserts that learning occurs through the construction of knowledge, with 'a prescription for how to teach'. They argue that knowledge construction happens through reading, listening to a lecture, watching a teacher demonstration – the students don't need to enact a process of constructing the knowledge first hand: it's a mental process; not a behavioural process. In the context of this myth-busting chapter, I'm arguing that student-centredness is inherent in the need for students to construct knowledge themselves, but this is about how they think, not about how they are required to behave in a lesson. Teacher-led instruction, formulated with student thinking at its core, is vital to the process – not exclusively, but often predominantly.

3. Education is always a blend of values and evidence. The case for mode B

My final line of reasoning is that a great education is not purely about the knowledge content that is accumulated; it is also about the enacted experience, the process of learning. In my view, there are many aspects of student activity and teacher-student engagement that are desirable simply because we value them as social constructs or because they enable teachers to be more expansive in the range of knowledge and experiences students encounter. I think is what Hmelo-Silver et al. refer to as 'valued practices'. In my book *The Learning Rainforest*, I refer to this set of learning activities as mode B teaching, contrasting it with the mainstay of teacher-led instruction that I call mode A teaching.

Over time, within a sequence of learning spanning weeks or even a whole school year, it's entirely legitimate to suggest that there is a balance to be found between mode A and mode B activities in order to provide the optimum curriculum diet, informed both by ideas about effective evidence-informed teaching and our values system. What might this include?

- **Collaborative learning:**

  As described by Robert Slavin (2010) and others, collaborative learning that is structured appropriately can yield significant learning gains. The gains can be explained in terms of the goal-setting aspect of the process whereby participants are motivated to ensure everyone in a collaborative group gains the knowledge needed to succeed in the task. They can also be explained in terms of cognitive load theory (Kirschner et al., 2018) where, in some situations, cognitive load for individuals can be reduced because it is shared between those involved.

  If we're clear to include pair work under the umbrella of collaborative learning, then I would suggest that it's hard to separate from instructional teaching because engaging students in paired discussions – airing their ideas, testing out hypotheses, engaging in peer assessment – is a highly valuable element in the repertoire of questioning techniques teachers can deploy during instruction.

  This is before we consider the social dimension and the broader dynamics of school life. It seems entirely uncontroversial that, as social beings, we should be setting up opportunities for students to work together in the pursuit of learning. Of course this will vary across different subject disciplines; but it is surely more a question of how often and how well we harness cooperative learning and for what purpose rather than whether we do it or not?

Clark et al. acknowledge this in their 2012 *American Educator* article: '[Explicit guidance] does not mean direct expository instruction all day every day. Small group and independent problems and projects can be effective – not as vehicles for making discoveries, but as a means of practicing recently learned content and skills.'

- **Open-ended tasks and projects**

There are numerous ways in which students can benefit from undertaking extended learning tasks where the form of response or the precise content is not predetermined; where students learn to make good choices about their learning. At a small scale this can start with the goal-free problem-solving approach described by John Sweller within his cognitive load theory (1988). Goal-free problems invite students to explore a scenario in a range of ways until various solutions are found and conceptual connections reinforced.

Going beyond this, the act of producing any form of extended writing involves making numerous decisions – form, content, line of argument, use of language. This can lead into much larger-scale projects where students engage in research, inquiry or investigative processes, leading to them acquiring knowledge that they can then express in a range of forms. In completing a successful project to a high standard, students will be making lots of choices; the entire process is highly student-centred. However, at the same time, through modelling certain elements, determining the success criteria and giving feedback, teacher instruction is also close at hand. Across a year, a student may only engage in a handful of these activities; but I have always found that, if expectations are set high, the outcomes can be phenomenal across a range of subjects.

- **Co-construction**

It is my experience that, given the right conditions, students can contribute valuable and valid ideas about their learning. When I hear teachers suggest that students can't really guide their learning – because how could they know enough to do so? – I almost feel sorry for them because it suggests they've never met the kind of students that I have who most certainly could. You only have to reflect on your own education to consider when, as a teenager growing up, you started to form legitimate academic interests and preferences; you started asking questions that you wanted answers to; you felt ready to make choices about what to study. Of course there are risks here – students left to their own devices might make terrible choices that cut off whole areas of study or lead to soft low-quality outcomes and shallow thinking. But, with teacher guidance – setting standards, guiding, nudging, directing – surely we have to concede that involving students in shaping their learning is not only possible but is desirable. This is the essence of co-construction.

Of course, this isn't going to be relevant when students are in a novice phase – it might not be appropriate or very extensive until much later in a student's school life. However, they will never learn to make good learning choices if they're never given the chance to make them. It's not something you can suddenly switch on; it has to be nurtured over time.

- **Education for citizenship**

  The final example I'll offer is around the idea that citizenship is something you do; it's not just something you learn about. How do we educate children to become engaged citizens? For sure, there will be the need for teacher-led instruction to ensure that key concepts are understood and remembered. However, if we're committed to teaching for citizenship, surely we need to include elements of the curriculum where students are required to gain knowledge and experience through more student-centred activities: debating; expressing opinions; organising themselves and others to present ideas. If students don't develop the sense that their voice matters at school, how are they going to find their voice as citizens in the wider world where the stakes are much higher? Citizenship isn't hypothetical, emanating from a knowledge base derived from instruction; it's lived; experienced. Student-centredness needs to be woven in.

Conclusion

My sense is that many people will read this and conclude that the myth isn't really a myth, that sensible teachers have always understood the value of teacher instruction and how this blends with notions of student-centredness. As ever, a myth isn't a myth to those who believe it. However, I am sure that out there in the world of education there are plenty of people advocating strongly for student-centredness almost as the antidote to the 'command and control' of teacher-led instruction. Similarly there are people who readily dismiss out of hand ideas about group work, projects and other expressions of student-centredness.

My view is that the opposition is false and I have presented the case via three lines of argument:

- The debate around minimally guided instruction gives prime importance to the need for teacher guidance, whist acknowledging that for more expert learners and as a form of practice, elements of small-group and independent work can play a valuable role.

- Successful responsive teaching is inherently student-centred if teachers are checking for understanding sufficiently and are ensuring that all students are both constructing knowledge securely and engaging in metacognitive thinking.

- Alongside mode A instructional teaching, there is a world of valued possibilities in mode B teaching that, when woven together, create a curriculum and a learning experience over time that is deeper and richer than we'd achieve through instructional teaching alone.

References

Clark, R., Kirschner, P. and Sweller, J. (2012) 'Putting students on the path to learning: the case for fully guided instruction', *American Educator* 36 (1) pp. 6–11.

Epiphany Learning (2016) [Tweet] 23 February. Retrieved from: www.bit.ly/2K8L0y9

Hattie, J. (2009) *Visible learning.* Abingdon: Routledge.

Hmelo-Silver, C. E., Duncan, R. G. and Chinn, C. A. (2007) 'Scaffolding and achievement in problem-based and inquiry learning: a response to Kirschner, Sweller, and Clark (2006)', *Educational Psychologist* 42 (2) pp. 99–107.

Kirschner, P. A., Sweller, J. and Clark, R. (2006) 'Why minimal guidance during instruction does not work: an analysis of the failure of constructivist, discovery, problem-based, experiential, and inquiry-based teaching', *Educational Psychologist* 41 (2) pp. 75–86.

Kirschner, P. A., Sweller, J., Kirschner, F. and Zambrano, J. (2018) 'From cognitive load theory to collaborative cognitive load theory', *International Journal of Computer-Supported Collaborative Learning* 13 (2) pp. 213–233.

Nuthall, G. (2007) *The hidden lives of learners.* Wellington: NZCER Press.

Rosenshine, B. (2012) 'Principles of instruction: research-based strategies that all teachers should know', *American Educator* 36 (1) pp. 12–19, 39.

Sherrington, T. (2017) *The learning rainforest: great teaching in real classrooms.* Woodbridge: John Catt Educational.

Shimamura, A. (2018) *MARGE: a whole-brain learning approach for students and teachers.* PDF available from www.bit.ly/2UEi1IB

Slavin, R. (2010) 'Co-operative learning: what makes group-work work?' in Dumont, H., Istance, D. and Benavides, F. (eds) *The nature of learning: using research to inspire practice*. Paris: OECD Publishing, pp. 161–178.

Sweller, J. (1988) 'Cognitive load during problem solving: effects on learning', *Cognitive Science* 12 (2) pp. 257–285.

Sweller, J., Kirschner, P. A. and Clark, R. (2007) 'Why minimally guided teaching techniques do not work: a reply to commentaries', *Educational Psychologist* 42 (2) pp. 115–121.

Wiliam, D. (2011) *Embedded formative assessment*. Bloomington, IN: Solution Tree Press.

Willingham, D. (2009) *Why don't students like school?* San Francisco, CA: Jossey-Bass.

Author bio-sketch:

Tom Sherrington is an education consultant and author. He writes the popular blog teacherhead.com and his books include *The Learning Rainforest, Great Teaching in Real Classrooms* and best-seller *Rosenshine's Principles in Action*. With 30 years' experience as a physics and maths teacher and school leader, including 11 years as a headteacher, Tom works with schools across the UK and around the world providing consultancy support on curriculum, assessment and improving the quality of teaching. He is a regular keynote speaker and contributor to conferences and education festivals.

ATTACHMENT MYTHS

BY ANDREW OLD

People have said many things about Andrew Old – often via Twitter, where he is @oldandrewuk. It is fair to say that his contributions to the education debate divide the so-called edu-Twitter community. But there is one thing that all parties can agree on – Andrew is never afraid to speak his mind and stand up for what he believes, whatever the cost of the personal backlash that may follow. His writings are provocative, thought-provoking, discussion-generating, and compulsive reading for all with an interest in the education of young people.

In this chapter, Andrew is again on fine form tackling what he perceives to be the myths and dangers surrounding attachment, behaviour, associated disorders and their proposed treatments. And with behaviour – alongside workload – often cited as the key reasons so many teachers leave our profession, it is a subject all educators have an interest in.

One of the enduring mysteries of the human condition is why we all sometimes do bad things. Among teachers, the cause of humanity's moral imperfections is particularly fiercely debated, as beliefs about why we do wrong inform our approaches to behaviour management. It often seems that almost every form of SEND has been associated with bad behaviour in children by somebody at some point. Even where a child's bad behaviour is not being speculatively linked to SEND, it may still be suggested that it is the result of their home environment, past traumas, their low self-esteem or the inadequacies of the curriculum. Over the years, many fanciful stories have been told about the causes of, and treatments for, behaviour problems. The celebrated radical headteacher A. S. Neill claimed that he had cured an 11-year-old boy of wanting to set fires by encouraging him to masturbate (Neill, 1990, pp. 190–191). Claims about the causes of bad behaviour in schools should always be scrutinised, and not assumed to be the result of unquestioned science delivered from unimpeachable authorities.

In recent years, ideas around attachment have been popularised as having a part to play in discussions about behaviour. The recent *Timpson Review of School Exclusion* (Department for Education, 2019) claimed that attachment was an underlying cause of poor behaviour (pp. 13, 68); recommended that training be given on attachment (pp. 13, 69); and repeatedly mentioned a condition called 'attachment disorder' (pp. 24, 27, 38, 60, 69, 71) that affects a child's chances of exclusion. It may surprise many teachers to learn that it has been disputed that attachment has any predictive power for behaviour; that there is no single medical condition known as 'attachment disorder'; and that serious concerns have been raised about the popularity of incorrect ideas about attachment and behaviour. While attachment has been studied by psychologists for decades (and is not a myth in its entirety), many of the ideas about attachment that are heard in schools and advocated by apparent experts are myths – and in some cases quite dangerous ones.

The science, as opposed to the mythology, of attachment is predominantly based on the work of researchers John Bowlby and Mary Ainsworth, an overview of which can be found in Bretherton (1992). Over several decades, from the 1940s to the 1980s, Bowlby contributed a body of work that predominantly looked at the relationship of an infant to its mother, and in particular the effects of separation and bereavement on development. Influenced by the research of ethologists into 'imprinting' (instinctive behaviours in animals and birds, adopted during sensitive periods of development, that are specific to particular individuals or groups of individuals), Bowlby formulated the idea of attachment, a deep emotional bond to a primary caregiver, taken to be the mother or a permanent mother substitute. This attachment would explain why infants might respond with anxiety to a stranger, or to a separation from the primary caregiver. Bowlby also credited this primary caregiver with orienting a child to the world and, he presumed, shaping the child's future emotional development.

Ainsworth made it possible to test some of Bowlby's ideas empirically, but also expanded the theory, setting much of the future direction in the study of attachment. Her observational studies of interactions between babies and their mothers gave rise to the classification of particular types of attachment behaviours as secure, avoidant and ambivalent (the latter two being types of insecure attachment). Insecure attachment, while sounding terrible, was found in a large proportion of cases and should not be assumed to imply a child had no emotional connection with their caregivers.

Over the decades, these theories have been revised and modified. Ainsworth's original model of attachment types has been revised to include 'disorganised attachment' where no consistent pattern of behaviour towards the caregiver has been observed. Mercer (2011) reviewed developments in attachment theory and found that many of the ideas Bowlby had about attachment, but not the existence of attachment, had been challenged. Ideas have changed enough that Mercer (2017), in a blog post covering similar territory to her earlier article, suggests that quoting Bowlby, to the exclusion of more modern work, is an indicator that somebody might have a perspective that is outside the mainstream view of attachment. It is in this area outside the mainstream – where there are a wide variety of myths, misconceptions and controversial ideas (often shared as uncontested facts) about attachment – that teachers have to be careful not to be misled.

The first warning to teachers about attachment myths is the most serious one, dealing with ideas that are not only wrong, but also extremely dangerous. There is an area of pseudoscience which promotes methods of therapy for treating alleged attachment problems but which has been implicated in the deaths of several children and the abuse of many others. This is described by Chaffin et al. (2006) (on behalf of The American Professional Society on the Abuse of Children), who warn of networks of attachment therapists, and adoptive or foster parents, who promote the ideas involved in 'controversial attachment therapies' despite widespread concern. According to the theories of attachment inherent in these controversial attachment therapies, children who have experienced adversity often have attachment problems that should be conceptualised as being the result of suppressed rage. These children are thought to be prevented from forming normal attachments by their rage, which also results in a lack of conscience, behaviour problems and difficulties trusting adults. They are seen as manipulative and in danger of becoming psychopaths.

The proponents of these controversial therapies, having invented an explanation for behaviour problems in children (particularly adopted children), also claim that their methods, rather than conventional therapies, will be the only effective treatment. Based on the theory that the affected child is manipulative and seeking control over adults, controversial attachment therapies can be deliberately cruel attempts to establish that the child is powerless, which can include: keeping the child at home away from others; setting them meaningless chores; making them sit motionless; completely controlling their intake of food, water and the use of a toilet. Attempts to encourage such children to release their rage may involve holding them down or lying on top of them for hours at a time as well as more coercive (but not physical) means.

While there is no scientific basis to these treatments – and as previously mentioned they have been implicated in child deaths – the proponents of these methods promote them enthusiastically to parents, particularly parents of adopted children. While I have never heard of these methods being adopted in schools, any teacher searching the internet, and particularly social media, for information about attachment may well find false information based on the theories related to these controversial and harmful treatments. Advocates of controversial attachment therapies can seem plausible and well informed. The *ChildMyths* blog (www.childmyths.blogspot.com) written by Jean Mercer, a retired professor of psychology, documents many of the strange and dangerous ideas spread by advocates of controversial attachment therapies and would be a useful resource for any teacher wishing to clarify the difference between mainstream and fringe theories of attachment.

While this dangerous fringe might not be influential in schools, one of the myths they hold to has spread into our education system. The belief that there is a single recognised condition called 'attachment disorder' that is responsible for a significant amount of poor behaviour in schools has been widely shared by teachers and educationalists. The *Timpson Review of School Exclusion* (Department for Education, 2019, p. 24) claimed that parents of excluded children they spoke to often said their child 'had additional needs such as SEN or attachment disorder, and many wrote that their child's exclusion was a symptom of the school's failure to understand and address their needs'. It also claimed (p. 27) that local authority staff had mentioned the need 'to work with children at risk of exclusion, particularly children with attachment disorder and SEN'. The report refers to behaviour 'triggered' by attachment disorder (p. 60) and to the need for staff with an understanding of attachment disorder (p. 69). While references like this are unusual in an official publication, they are not uncommon among educators on social media. Back in 2015, I first noticed that talk of attachment disorder was becoming common in schools, and I found several examples that I detailed in a blog post (Old, 2015). I found one blog post where a school SENCO (special education needs coordinator) talked about a class of poorly behaved children claiming, 'Many of the children who attend this class show behaviours which are typical of, amongst other things, an Attachment Disorder.' In another blog post, an SLE in behaviour suggested that 'violent behaviour' and swearing and spitting were plausible presentations of attachment disorder.

Woolgar and Scott (2014) found that:

> In many child services across health, education and social care, 'attachment disorder' is a popular description and explanation for complex presentations of children who have been neglected or maltreated

and is frequently used to describe fostered and adopted children. Very often the use of this term bears little resemblance to the established diagnostic systems, nor indeed to attachment theory as conceptualised by Bowlby. Its misuse can lead professionals to overlook commoner and more treatable conditions, to the detriment of the children.

It is not always clear whether those who claim that 'attachment disorder' is a common cause of poor behaviour are misinformed about existing, recognised conditions, or referring to a condition that does not exist. The mainstream diagnostic manuals do not list a single disorder known as 'attachment disorder'. According to Woolgar and Scott (2014, p. 2), DSM-IV-TR describes two subtypes of reactive attachment disorder (RAD) and ICD-10 has equivalent diagnoses of RAD and disinhibited attachment disorder (DAD). These are thought to be very rare, even in high-risk samples, and should only be diagnosed in cases where a child has experienced pathogenic care before the age of five and should not be assumed in all cases of trauma, adoption or difficulties in the child-carer relationship. Barth et al. (2005) echo many of the same arguments, but also argues that even RAD may be overdiagnosed because of an overconfidence in the explanatory power of attachment theory. According to Chaffin et al. (2006, p. 81):

> Although RAD may underlie occasional behavior problems among children who are severely maltreated, several much more common and demonstrably treatable diagnoses – with substantial research evidence linking them to a history of maltreatment – may better account for many of these difficulties. Therefore, it should not be assumed that RAD underlies all or even most of the behavioral and emotional problems seen in foster children, adoptive children, or children who are maltreated.

For this reason, I would argue that teachers should not attempt to explain students' poor behaviour in terms of attachment disorders. Nor is there any reason to assume that a student with RAD or DAD would be poorly behaved in school. DSM-IV-TR makes no mention of any symptom that would be obviously associated with poor behaviour in school. The ICD-10 does accept that emotional disturbance may result in aggression in some cases of RAD and 'depending on circumstances there may also be associated emotional or behavioural disturbance' with DAD, but neither suggests that behaviour problems in school are inevitable or simply to be expected in all cases. Both diagnostic manuals require that symptoms appear before the age of five for such a diagnosis to be accepted. The idea that a diagnosis of RAD or DAD is clearly connected to violent or anti-social behaviour seems to draw on the fringe advocates of 'attachment therapy' and their belief in the underlying rage of children rather than any mainstream diagnoses. According to Chaffin et al. (2006, p. 81), 'Although RAD may underlie occasional behavior problems among children who are severely maltreated, several much more common and demonstrably treatable diagnoses – with substantial research evidence linking them to a history of maltreatment – may better account for many of these difficulties.' Even if a teacher was to be sure a student did have RAD or DAD, there is no real consensus on treatment, and certainly no evidence-based approach to teaching students with those disorders that is different to that recommended for any other students.

There is the question of whether attachment theory itself could be of use to the teacher. It does not seem implausible that an early years teacher might be able to interpret the behaviour of very young children towards their closest caregivers in light of the study of attachment. However, there have been suggestions that attachment theory might be highly relevant to understanding children's behaviour more generally. A 2018 article in *Schools Week* was entitled 'Train all teachers in attachment issues, says trauma expert' (Staufenberg, 2018) and reported that:

> Emma Gater, the principal of the Meadows Primary Academy in Stoke-on-Trent, said understanding attachment theory 'utterly transformed' her school.

> First, a pupil's feelings are recognised, validated and labelled, then the appropriate limits on behaviour are explained, and future behaviour strategies are discussed.

> Her school wouldn't suit prospective teachers who prefer a 'punitive' system of behaviour management, she claimed. According to one staff member, emotion coaching 'ensures the children do not reflect the negativity shown towards them in a more traditional approach'.

Narratives that claim that behaviour can be managed with positivity alone and without the need for sanctions are not uncommon in education. However, how plausible is it that attachment theory explains children's classroom behaviour?

Much of the theory applies to the specific context of very young children and their primary caregiver. While the theory has developed to encompass more than one caregiver, it is not clear that it describes the relationships children have with adults at school, who, by the very nature of their job, are always intended to be temporary fixtures in a child's life. The most important attachments in a child's life are likely to be with their immediate family. There is no obvious reason to think that schools have a place in either judging or replacing those relationships.

Could it be possible that attachment theory may help explain behaviours in older children that could be rooted in their early childhood? Mercer (2011, p. 34) suggests that one of the tenets of Bowlby's theory, which is now highly contested, is the idea that 'early attachment experiences play an essential part in determining later social behavior' and identifies various criticisms that have been made of the idea. It is disputed as to whether attachment behaviour can be observed over time as behaviour changes as children age. There has been criticism of 'infant determinism', the assumption that events in early life have a greater causal power than those which occur later. Mercer (2017) also indicates that modern researchers would not share Bowlby's low estimate of the effects of genes on behaviour.

Claims about the effects of insecure attachment have come under particular scrutiny. Meins (2017) gives multiple examples of policy makers claiming that early insecure attachment leads to harm and poor outcomes later in life, but then observes, 'The fact is that there's no strong evidence for parent-child attachment in infancy predicting anything much about children's later development.' While correlations have been observed between attachment types and some later behaviours, Meins argues that there is a very complex picture that cannot and should not be simplified to the idea that insecure attachment is a cause of problems in later life. The correlations vary depending on gender and the type of insecure attachment considered. Moreover, studies that are quoted as offering an insight into the effects of attachment might observe a young child's relationship with just one parent, or at the other extreme look at the totality of an adolescent's or an adult's relationships. It would be a mistake to draw conclusions from combining such disparate research. In summary:

> Insecure attachment is being pathologised and vilified. It is not abnormal – at least 39 per cent of us are insecurely attached. Different types of attachment simply reflect the kind of individual differences you'd expect to see in any aspect of children's early development. People are perfectly happy with variation in toddlers' height, weight and ability to walk and talk, but don't want variation in attachment relationships. Secure attachment is wrongly being set up as a benchmark for all toddlers to attain.

A final consideration comes from the possibility that attachment theory itself may not be as generally applicable as is often believed. Over the decades since Bowlby and Ainsworth's original research, researchers have come to question at length the extent to which their observations are true across different cultures. Quinn and Mageo (2013) edited an entire book exploring this question. There appear to be cultures that do not demonstrate well the types of attachment that attachment theory describes, but which nevertheless allow children to develop into emotionally healthy adults. If anthropologists are to be believed, the biggest attachment myth of all may be the idea that attachment theory describes universal human norms, rather than just the features of child-rearing in some Western societies.

As educators of children, we will always want to understand children better and we will always be interested in any knowledge that will inform our efforts to manage behaviour. Sometimes, however, we are fed inaccurate information and encouraged to interpret our experience in the classroom in light of it. The concept of attachment may explain some of the behaviour of very young children in some cultures. Nevertheless, we should be suspicious when claims go beyond that. We should be very suspicious when the behaviour of older children is explained in terms of their earliest experiences. We should be extremely suspicious when a single disorder is suggested as an explanation for a vast array of motivations and behaviour. Most importantly, if anybody suggests they have radical and extreme treatments for disordered children that, while popular in some quarters on the internet, are unsupported by mainstream medicine or psychology, we should not give them even the slightest foothold in our schools.

References

Barth, R. P., Crea, T. M., John, K., Thoburn, J. and Quinton, D. (2005) 'Beyond attachment theory and therapy: towards sensitive and evidence-based interventions with foster and adoptive families in distress', *Child & Family Social Work* 10 (4) pp. 257–268.

Bretherton, I. (1992) 'The origins of attachment theory: John Bowlby and Mary Ainsworth', *Developmental Psychology* 28 (5) pp. 759–775.

Chaffin, M., Hanson, R., Saunders, B. E., Nichols, T., Barnett, D., Zeanah, C., Berliner, L., Egeland, B., Newman, E., Lyon, T., LeTourneau, E. and Miller-Perrin, C. (2006) Report of the APSAC task force on attachment therapy, reactive attachment disorder, and attachment problems, *Child Maltreatment* 11 (1) pp. 76–89.

Department for Education (2019) *Timpson review of school exclusion.* London: The Stationery Office.

Meins, E. (2017) 'Overrated: the predictive power of attachment', *The Psychologist* 30, pp. 20–24.

Mercer, J. (2011) 'Attachment theory and its vicissitudes: toward an updated theory', *Theory & Psychology* 21 (1) pp. 25–45.

Mercer, J. (2017) 'Referencing John Bowlby: not your grandpa's attachment theory any more', *ChildMyths* [Blog], 29 November. Retrieved from: www.bit.ly/2K8oLbF

Neill, A. S. (1990) *Summerhill.* London: Penguin.

Old, A. (2015) 'The latest SEN fad diagnosis: attachment disorder', *Scenes from the Battleground* [Blog], 29 June. Retrieved from: www.bit.ly/2LU79Cy

Quinn, N. and Mageo, J. (eds) (2013) *Attachment reconsidered: cultural perspectives on a Western theory*. New York, NY: Palgrave Macmillan.

Staufenberg, J. (2018) 'Train all teachers in attachment issues, says trauma expert', *Schools Week* [Online], 27 August. Retrieved from: www.bit.ly/2T1U4YC

Woolgar, M. and Scott, S. (2014) 'The negative consequences of over-diagnosing attachment disorders in adopted children: the importance of comprehensive formulations', *Clinical Child Psychology and Psychiatry* 19 (3) pp. 355–366.

Author bio-sketch:

Andrew Old is a maths teacher and blogger based in the West Midlands. He has spoken at many researchED conferences. His master's dissertation was on evidence and ideology in SEN policy. He blogs at teachingbattleground.wordpress.com.

DON'T SHOOT THE MYTHBUSTER
BY HARRY FLETCHER-WOOD

I have long admired the work of Harry Fletcher-Wood. He writes with a clarity, a humility and a common-sense approach that are rare in educators, and his work with regard to formative assessment and diagnostic questions was extremely influential in my early forays into that area.

Harry is the perfect person to bring this book to a close by focusing on one area we have neglected so far – how to change people's beliefs and practice. It is all well and good identifying these myths, but even with a convincing argument supported by a wealth of evidence, humans remain particularly resistant to change. Here Harry offers some practical guidance for helping you help your colleagues to see the light!

Combating education myths effectively means persuading colleagues to change their beliefs and their practice.

Consider the following situations: how should you respond?

- You're a guest at an initial teacher training session. The presenter has just begun to explain learning styles.

- A senior colleague is explaining that the organisation's new approach to improving employee performance is based on the 'evidence' that learning on the job is 70% informal, 20% from others and 10% from formal training. (This is a myth: see De Bruyckere et al., 2015)

- You're leading a training session and have just described dual coding. A teacher misinterprets this as validating learning styles.

- Your colleague is explaining a scheme of work they've planned for the department. Their planning has been informed by several education myths.

I've been in all these situations. I'm not sure I've dealt with any of them well. One reason is put best by Brent Maddin at Arizona State University: 'Being right is not an effective persuasion strategy.' In each case I'd done the reading and I knew the evidence, but that didn't mean my case was clear, patient or persuasive. More importantly, what mattered was not winning the argument, but changing my colleagues' beliefs and practice. Recalling how I responded to the four situations described above, even my most cautious, careful and persuasive response – a carefully worded email explaining why I thought we needed to avoid the myth – never got an answer. I failed entirely as a mythbuster.

It's not surprising that I struggled: the mythbuster's message is unwelcome. When we try to dissuade people from education myths, we're telling colleagues and friends they're wrong. They're not just wrong about the capital of Paraguay; they're wrong about how they plan and teach: they were wrong to plan using learning styles, wrong to prioritise memorable experiences over semantic memory, wrong to provide massed practice rather than interleaving. We're suggesting that they've been wasting their time and harming their students' learning; we're implying that they're a bad teacher or a leader. Will they thank us? Adam Smith (2006, p. 101) has the answer:

> A messenger who brings bad news is disagreeable to us, whereas we feel a sort of gratitude to the man who brings us good news. For a moment we regard them as the authors of our good fortune (in one case) and of our bad fortune (in the other), looking at them rather as though they had really brought about the events that they only report to us.

Even if we set aside the unwelcome nature of our news, education myths may be particularly hard to shift. They are often:

- Intuitively appealing – the importance of memorable experiences seems clear from our own experience, even though, as Clare Sealy notes, semantic memory is more powerful.

- Ideologically rooted – many myths rest more on beliefs than evidence: Greg Ashman notes the links between differentiation and individualism, for example.

- Concealing a grain of truth – a myth is often an accurate idea which has mutated through accountability systems or cargo cult approaches, as Mark Enser explains in his chapter.

- Hard to pin down – Greg Ashman notes the risk of woolly terms: if I suggest that something is a myth, I may be told that I don't understand it.

- Resistant to evidence – Bob and Elizabeth Bjork note that people continue to prefer massing to interleaving, even when they are presented with evidence of their own success with massing, and the general rule.

Letting sleeping myths lie is socially easier than combating them. As Mark Enser notes, however, teachers' thinking and planning is based on their knowledge and beliefs – true or false – about how students learn. What's a would-be mythbuster to do?

This chapter suggests six steps to combat education myths, based on my experiences and the evidence around addressing misconceptions. Throughout, I've imagined I'm working with Frank, who has just told me that he caters for visual, auditory and kinaesthetic learners in his lessons. I've chosen to focus on learning styles, not because it's the most common education myth (although 18% of English teachers in one recent survey said they were differentiating using them – Teacher Tapp, 2018), but because it's the myth I've encountered most often (I was asked whether it was true by a teacher last week) and therefore the myth I've had the most practice trying to discourage. Nonetheless, because learning styles share the features of a myth described above (intuitively appealing, resistant to evidence, and so on), this approach should apply whatever myth you are seeking to bust.

1) Pinpoint the misconception

Stephen Covey suggests that we should '**seek first to understand, then to be understood**'. He notes our tendency to 'rush in, to fix things up with good advice' and our failure to 'take the time to diagnose, to really, deeply understand the problem first' (Covey, 2003, p. 237, emphasis original). I may think Frank believes in learning styles, but I may have misinterpreted his description. I need to know more about what he believes: the contours and limits of the myth, whether he's aware of the evidence for or against it. This is crucial because sometimes myths look very similar to truths: visual, auditory and kinaesthetic learning can be confused with dual coding – providing both verbal and visual presentation and study opportunities, which has a good body of evidence behind it (Pashler et al., 2007). I also want to know how it's affecting his teaching, so I'll ask him for an example of how he uses this idea in lessons. This will show me how big a role the myth is playing in his planning. It will also provide a concrete example which we can return to and discuss in light of our subsequent discussion about the evidence for learning styles.

To test whether I've pinpointed the misconception, my initial goal will be to adopt Daniel Dennett's suggested first step in disagreeing with someone: 'Attempt to re-express your target's position so clearly, vividly, and fairly that your target says, "Thanks, I wish I'd thought of putting it that way"' (Popova, 2014). I might summarise Frank's approach in this way: 'So when you plan, you try to make sure you have a variety of activities, including bits which students have to look at and which they have to listen to?'

At this stage, the mythbuster may ask:

- 'Can you tell me a bit more about this idea?'
- 'How does your planning reflect this?'
- 'Can you tell me a recent time you've used this in a lesson?'
- 'So, am I right to say that your approach is…?'

2) Acknowledge the merits of the myth

Before I dive into my refutation, I will take a moment to follow Dennett's second and third suggested steps (Popova, 2014):

- 'You should list any points of agreement (especially if they are not matters of general or widespread agreement).'
- 'You should mention anything you have learned from your target.'

I hope to convey that I'm learning, that I don't have all the answers, and that this is a discussion between professionals, not a lecture from me. This may prove tricky, but there is almost always some aspect of our colleagues' work that we can benefit from. I might say: 'I've always struggled to maintain students' full attention in the afternoons too. I really like the way you've tried to encourage attention while still maintaining a focus on the learning.' Alternatively, I may appreciate the importance of Frank's values and beliefs, which are supporting the myth – for example: 'I really respect the trouble you're taking to ensure every student gets the chance to grasp the key ideas.'

At this stage, the mythbuster may say:

- 'I see why this could be helpful – I've found that my students appreciate a similar approach, when I…'
- 'I think what you've described is a powerful idea…'
- 'I've faced the same problem, and I think the way you've approached this is potentially powerful because…'

3) Present the evidence persuasively

Once I'm clear what Frank thinks, and I've expressed my appreciation for his efforts, I'll present some of the evidence about the myth, humbly and gently. This is made harder because there's likely to be evidence I've read which Frank hasn't, and vice versa. Being persuasive about things Frank hasn't read is tough: there may be 'loads of studies' and I may have 'read all around this', but telling Frank all this evidence exists does little to convey what it actually says. My description of systematic reviews or the methodology of meta-analyses may be alienating or confusing. We may debate at cross purposes, each referring to studies the other hasn't read – this may tempt Frank to conclude that evidence contributes little, because you can 'find a study to prove anything', 'researchers can't really help teachers', or he knows 'what works for my students'. For example, I could quote the conclusions of the authoritative review on learning styles:

> At present, there is no adequate evidence base to justify incorporating learning styles assessments into general educational practice. Thus, limited education resources would better be devoted to adopting other educational practices that have a strong evidence base, of which there are an increasing number. (Pashler et al., 2008, p.105)

But unless Frank knows how and why they came to this conclusion, or he's read the paper, he may not find this persuasive.

A more productive approach might be to take him through the steps which the researchers took, so Frank joins them on their path to their conclusion. In this review, the researchers (Pashler et al., 2008):

- Identified the kind of research which would provide evidence for learning styles. You would have to, for example, take students who were deemed 'visual' and 'auditory' learners, teach some 'visual' learners 'visually' and 'auditory' learners 'auditorily', and then find a significant benefit for 'visual' teaching for 'visual' learners.

- Searched for studies which met these criteria.

- Reviewed what they found, concluding that 'although the literature on learning styles is enormous, very few studies have even used an experimental methodology capable of testing the validity of learning styles applied to education'. The researchers 'found virtually no evidence' to validate the theory of learning styles, and, of studies with appropriate methods, 'several found results that flatly contradict [the hypothesis]' (Pashler et al., 2008, p. 105).

Taking Frank through the steps the researchers took may show the logic and force of their conclusions more powerfully than a bald summary of their conclusions.

At this stage, the mythbuster may:

- Mention any major reviews of the myth.

- Describe the research process and findings.

- Explain a specific study which tested the idea compellingly.

4) Use bridging analogies to challenge misconceptions

Presenting the evidence, however, is only a foundation for our effort to influence Frank's beliefs and practices. It may encourage him to learn more about the topic, but it is usually insufficient, on its own, to convince him to change. A powerful approach to targeting misconceptions is the bridging analogy. Bridging analogies show people how an existing correct belief exemplifies the idea we want them to grasp (Luciarello and Naff, no date). For example, let's say students hold the misconception that a medieval king had total power and could do whatever he wanted. I begin with a known situation: students know that, while the headteacher is in charge, they cannot watch every student every minute – chewing gum may be banned, but it still circulates around the school. I then analogise: if a headteacher doesn't enjoy dictatorial power in a community of one thousand, how can a king enjoy such power in a community of a couple of million?

In the same way, I can begin with practical, unambiguous examples and bridge to help Frank appreciate the misconception. For example, I might highlight the importance of:

- Using maps in geography (even for 'auditory' learners)
- Practising speaking in French (even for 'visual' learners)
- Moving in sports lessons (even for 'visual' and 'auditory' learners)

From these simple, concrete and (hopefully) uncontroversial examples, I can suggest a conclusion: the best way to teach students reflects what we are trying to teach, not students' purported learning styles.

At this stage, the mythbuster can:

- Offer simple, concrete and uncontroversial examples.
- Link these examples to highlight the underlying problems with the myth.

5) Offer something better

Trying to extinguish undesirable behaviours is challenging: it can be more effective to replace them with more desirable behaviours. For example, it's easier to stop smoking if people use a nicotine replacement patch, or an e-cigarette, than if they simply try to stop (Silagy et al., 2002). This matters – first, because asking Frank to 'stop thinking about learning styles' in his planning leaves a vacuum: how should he judge what makes a good activity, or try to meet different students' needs?; and second, I want to help Frank teach more effectively, not just to bust myths: I need to offer Frank simple, evidence-informed ideas which will help him plan better. I may discuss the working memory model with him, noting the importance of carefully selecting the key ideas in the lesson and removing extraneous cognitive load which may distract students. Or I may describe dual coding, and the ways in which information presented visually and verbally may be more comprehensible and memorable to students.

At this stage, the mythbuster can:

- Introduce teaching principles which are likely to prove useful.

- Highlight similarities and differences between the new idea and the myth.

- Demonstrate the advantages of the new idea.

6) Turn abstract ideas into concrete changes

My goal is to change how Frank teaches. Just persuading him the working memory model has merits is insufficient; I need to work through these ideas so that he uses them in his teaching. So, I will work through the implications of these new ideas for an upcoming lesson. For example, we might discuss ways to limit extraneous cognitive load by removing distractions in a lesson Frank has planned. The implications may go beyond Frank's next lesson: he may have questions about how this fits with school policy or how he conveys a new approach to students or parents. I may also highlight how a new approach diminishes Frank's workload or solves other problems. A single conversation may not be sufficient to change colleagues' approaches for good; ideally, I will follow up later. What I hope to do, however, is open Frank's eyes to fresh ideas and evidence and help Frank to apply them, showing their value for him and his students.

At this stage, the mythbuster may say:

- Shall we look at a future lesson and see how these ideas might fit it?

- Is there anything which would stop you from using this approach?

- Can we catch up about how this has worked next week?

Conclusion

There is no perfect approach to persuading people that an education myth is not real. I think I've failed more often than not, sometimes causing offence in the process. Being right was never sufficient.

Any time we encounter a misconception, I'd suggest answering these six questions:

1. What does my colleague really believe?

2. What merit does their argument have?

3. How can I convey what the evidence suggests persuasively?

4. How can I bridge from true beliefs to correct the misconceptions?

5. What can I offer that's a better replacement for the misconception?

6. How can I help my colleague to change their practice?

I wouldn't claim the six steps suggested here are the perfect recipe: which ones are applicable and usable will depend on our roles and relationship. I would claim that this approach is more promising than what I've done in the past. If you take one idea from this chapter, I hope it's this: 'Being right is not an effective persuasion strategy.' The mythbuster is right: they use their knowledge to help their colleagues teach more effectively.

References

Covey, S. (2003) *The seven habits of highly effective people*. Carlsbad, CA: Hay House.

De Bruyckere, P., Kirschner, P., Hulshof, C. (2015) *Urban myths about learning and education*. Academic Press: London.

Lucariello, J. and Naff, D. (no date) 'How do I get my students over their alternative conceptions (misconceptions) for learning?', *American Psychological Association* [Website]. Retrieved from: www.bit.ly/2Ymx5gL

Pashler, H., Bain, P., Bottge, B., Graesser, A., Koedinger, K., McDaniel, M. and Metcalfe, J. (2007) *Organizing instruction and study to improve student learning* (NCER 2007-2004). Washington, DC: National Center for Education Research, Institute of Education Sciences, US Department of Education.

Pashler, H., McDaniel, M., Rohrer, D., Bjork, R. (2008) 'Learning styles: concepts and evidence', *Psychological Science in the Public Interest* 9 (3) pp. 105–119.

Popova, M. (2014) 'How to criticize with kindness: philosopher Daniel Dennett on the four steps to arguing intelligently', *Brain Pickings* [Blog], 28 March. Retrieved from: www.bit.ly/2yACXDv

Silagy, C., Lancaster, T., Stead, L., Mant, D., Fowler, G. (2002) 'Nicotine replacement therapy for smoking cessation', *Cochrane Database of Systematic Reviews* 2002 (4).

Smith, A. (2006) *The theory of moral sentiments*. 6th edn. Mineola, NY: Dover Philosophical Classics.

Teacher Tapp (2018) 'What teachers tapped last week #31 – 30th April 2018', *Teacher Tapp* [Website]. Retrieved from: www.bit.ly/2OBvwqG

Author bio-sketch:
Harry Fletcher-Wood has worked in schools in Japan, India and London, teaching history, organising university applications and leading teacher development. He now works at Ambition Institute, where he leads the Fellowship in Teacher Education. He blogs regularly at improvingteaching.co.uk, tweets sporadically as @hfletcherwood. Responsive Teaching: Cognitive Science and Formative Assessment in Practice is out now.